AF684632

TEXAS LABOR LAWS

Gulf Publishing Company
Book Division
Houston, London, Paris, Tokyo

Third Edition

TEXAS LABOR LAWS

Joan M. McCrea

TEXAS LABOR LAWS Third Edition

Copyright © 1978 by Joan M. McCrea
Houston, Texas. All rights reserved.
Printed in the United States of America.
This book, or parts thereof, may not be reproduced in any form without permission of the publisher.

Library of Congress
Catalog Card Number:
77-90788
ISBN 0-87201-414-2

Contents

Preface

This guide to labor laws in Texas is intended as an aid for students, workers, small employers, local employee organizations, and other laymen who do not have ready access to the statutes affecting workers, employees, and unions. More detailed information is always available from any office of the state or federal agency administering the law.

This is an expanded and amended version of *Texas Labor Laws,* first published in 1971. Far-reaching changes have recently been enacted in the areas of collective bargaining for police and firemen; extension of coverage of unemployment insurance, social security, minimum wage laws, and workers' compensation; federal legislation on occupational health and safety; and equal rights for women. In addition to these amendments, a chapter on employer taxes has been added.

Labor law in the United States results directly from the shift of the American economy from an agricultural to an industrial polarization. With industrialization came the development of labor unions and the need for legal definitions, guidelines, and safeguards.

The legal status of labor unions has evolved from repressive common-law decisions of the nineteenth century, through sympathetic New Deal legislation of the 1930s, to a balanced power philosophy as expressed in congressional acts of 1947 and 1959. Federal law encourages union organization and collective bargaining, while protecting the rights of individual workers and of the general public.

Labor legislation has become so comprehensive yet so detailed, so multifarious yet so particularized, so universally applicable yet so inaccessible to nonlawyers, that workers and small employers need help in understanding how its provisions work.

Many persons have provided helpful ideas, criticism, and corrections. I owe a special debt to the following state officials who have read and corrected portions of the manuscript: Jerry Belcher, Executive Director, Texas Industrial Accident Board; J.W. Burcham, Unemployment Insurance Director, Texas Employment Commission; Arnold Garza, Texas Department of Agriculture; Walter G. Martin, Director, Division of Occupational Safety; and Dallas Sasser, Jr., Director, Labor Division, Texas Department of Labor and Standards. I am grateful to Ms. Charlene Ferguson for her patient and efficient typing of the manuscript. Time for research and writing was made possible through a grant from the Organized Research Fund of the Graduate School of The University of Texas at Arlington.

June 1978

Legal Annotations

Civ. App., 1958—The case was decided by the Court of Civil Appeals in 1958.

Comm. App., 1922—The case was decided by the Commission of Appeals in 1922.

Cr. R.—*Texas Criminal Reports,* series of decisions of Court of Criminal Appeals. 151 Cr. R. 343 refers to volume 151, page 343.

Galv., 1941—The case was decided by the Court of Civil Appeals in Galveston in 1941.

H.B. 395, L. 1963—House Bill 3951 passed by the Legislature in 1963.

16 LRRM 634—*Labor Relations Reference Manual,* Volume 16, page 634.

Op. Atty. Gen.—*Digest of Opinions of the Attorney General of Texas,* published annually, and numbered consecutively throughout the tenure of each office. M-433 refers to the 433rd opinion of Attorney General Crawford Martin.

P.C. 1613—*Vernon's Annotated Penal Code of the State of Texas,* Article 1613.

R.C.S. Art. 5152—*Vernon's Revised Civil Statutes of the State of Texas,* Article 5152. Most of the civil statutes on labor are contained in volume 15 of R.C.S., Articles 5144-5221.

S.W. and S.W.2d—*Southwestern Reporter,* first series (1886 to 1927) and second series (1927 to date). Volume number precedes, and page number follows the citation.

148 T 434—*Texas Reports,* Volume 148, page 434.

323 U.S. 516—*United States Supreme Court Reports,* Volume 323, page 516.

1

Laws Relating to Labor Relations

Collective Bargaining

The growth and development of labor unions is characteristic of the change from an agricultural to an industrial economy. The legal status of unions in the United States has changed from repressive common-law decisions of the nineteenth century, through positive encouragement of the New Deal legislation of the 1930s (epitomized in the National Labor Relations [Wagner] Act of 1935), to the policy of balanced power characterized by the Labor Management Relations (Taft-Hartley) Act of 1947 and the Labor Management Reporting and Disclosure (Landrum-Griffin) Act of 1959. The substance of federal law is that union organization and collective bargaining should be encouraged, but also that the rights of individual workers and of the general public should be protected.

The federal laws apply to employers and employees who are engaged in interstate commerce. The interpretation of interstate commerce has been so broadened during the past thirty years that all transportation and communication enterprises and most manufacturing and distribution concerns are covered under federal law. Many states enacted "little" Wagner Acts and "little" Taft-Hartley Acts as a consequence of the federal acts. The area of jurisdiction of state labor laws is in small retail-sales establishments, in services, and in agriculture, which is generally excluded from federal labor laws.

The right of workers to organize and form trade unions was established in Texas in 1899 (R.C.S. Art. 5152).

A later court decision clearly established the right of workers to organize. In Sheehan v. Levy, 238 S.W. 900 (Comm. App., 1922), the Supreme Court of Texas stated that the law authorizes

> organizations such as labor unions, and give(s) them the right, within certain bounds, to act together to promote their general welfare. Not only does the law of Texas so permit, but other authorities hold that laboring people may organize for the purpose of promoting their common welfare, elevating their standard of skill, and advancing and maintaining their wages, fixing the hours of labor and the rate of wages paid, obtaining employment for their members.

The right to individual or collective bargaining for terms and conditions of employment is also guaranteed. The Texas Right to Work Act of 1947 provides as follows:

> Section 1. The inherent right of a person to work and bargain freely with his employer, individually or collectively, for terms and conditions of his employment shall not be denied or infringed by law, or by any organization of whatever nature.
>
> Section 2. No person shall be denied employment on account of membership or nonmembership in a labor union (R.C.S. Art. 5207a).

These rights, however, are not inevitable. No state law requires an employer to recognize or bargain with a union representing his employees. The law merely states that trade unions and collective bargaining are not illegal, without requiring an employer to bargain with a union (Flenoy v. Yarbrough, 318 S.W. 2d 15 [Civ. App. 1958]).

The law which prohibits licensed vocational nurses from membership in unions that advocate the right to strike (R.C.S. Art. 4528c-10A) is unconstitutional (Op. Atty. Gen. No. H-389 [1974]).

Right to Work Law

Federal law purposely left an important loophole for state determination with respect to the "union shop." The Taft-Hartley Act of 1947 made the "closed shop" illegal by making it an unfair labor practice to require in a collective agreement that the employer hire only union members. An agreement to require the "union shop," whereby all employees must join the union, usually after a probationary period, was permitted. However, in an exception to the principle that federal law supersedes state law, the act permitted state laws on the union shop to apply even to workers in interstate commerce. Nineteen states, including Texas, outlaw the union shop.

The Texas Right to Work Act of 1947 provides that every person has an inherent right to work and bargain freely with his employer, either individually or collectively, for terms and conditions of his employment. This right cannot be infringed by law or by any organization, even a labor union. Membership or nonmembership in a labor union cannot be used as a condition of employment. Any contract which requires that employees shall be , shall not be, or remain members of a labor union, is illegal—"null and void and against public policy" (R.C.S. Art. 5207a). An attorney general opinion dated November 16, 1951, found that a hiring-hall provision in a union contract was permissible when it did not require an exclusive closed-shop arrangement.

The Union Security Act of 1951 provides for enforcement of the right-to-work law by making union-shop agreements a conspiracy in restraint of trade (R.C.S. Art. 7428-1). The "agency shop" contract, wherein nonunion employees are required to pay union dues as a fee for services of the union as their agent, was ruled unlawful by the attorney general of Texas in 1961 (Op. Atty. Gen. No. WW-1018 [1961]).

Railroad and airline employees, who are covered under the Railway Labor Act rather than under the Federal Labor Management Relations Act, are not restricted by the Texas Right to Work Act. The Texas Court of Appeals held that the union-shop amendment to the Federal Railway Labor Act permitting a union shop contract superseded state laws (International Association of Machinists v. Sandsberry, 277 S.W. 2d 776 [Civ. App. 1955]).

Texas right to work laws do not apply when the employees' predominant job situs is a federal enclave (Vincent *et al.* v. General Dynamics Corp., *et al.*, CA 4-2221, 1977; or the job situs is on the high seas Oil, Chemical and Atomic Workers Union v. Mobil Oil Corp., S.C. 74-1254, 1976).

Blacklisting

Blacklisting, defined as publicizing the name of a former employee so as to prevent his obtaining another job, has been prohibited since 1907 (R.C.S. Art. 5196a). This technique was used to discourage union organization, since a man fired for union activity in one plant could be effectively barred from future employment elsewhere. The law also prohibits discrimination against any applicant for employment because of his having participated in a strike (R.C.S. Art. 5196-6). However, it does not prohibit an employer from furnishing a written truthful statement of the reason for discharge. An employer is prohibited from discharging, disciplining, or blacklisting any employee for failure to do business at any store or place (R.C.S. Art. 5196g).

Fire and Police Employee Relations

The Texas Fire and Police Employee Relations Act of 1973 provides that firefighters and policemen have the right to organize and bargain collectively with their employer as to wages, hours, and working conditions. Political subdivisions in Texas must provide compensation and other employment conditions which are substantially the same as those prevailing in the private sector for jobs which require similar skills, ability, and training. Collective bargaining is recognized as a fair and practical method for determining wages and working conditions. Work stoppages and slowdowns are prohibited, and a system of binding arbitration is provided as an alternative to strikes.

The provisions of the act may be adopted by local option. The lesser of 5% or 20,000 of the qualified voters in any political subdivision must sign a petition requesting an election. An election must be held within 60 days after the petition is filed. The question submitted to the voters must state:

> "FOR or AGAINST" the following: Adoption of the state law applicable to "firefighters and policemen" or "firefighters" or "policemen," (whichever shall be applicable), which establishes collective bargaining when a majority of the affected employers favor representation by an employees' association and which preserves the prohibition of strikes and lockouts and provides penalties therefore.

The act becomes effective in the locality within 30 days after the beginning of the next fiscal year following the election.

An association selected by a majority of the paid firefighters or sworn full-time paid policemen must be recognized as the exclusive bargaining agent for all the firefighters or policemen. In the event of disagreement on election procedures, either party may request the American Arbitration Association to conduct the election.

The public employer and the association are required to meet at reasonable times and to bargain in good faith, with respect to wages, hours, and working conditions. Either party may request mediation to reach a voluntary agreement. Whenever wages are involved, the association must notify the public employer at least 120 days before the end of the current fiscal operating budget. All deliberations are open to the public.

When an impasse is reached in the collective bargaining process, (i.e., when the parties do not reach agreement within 60 days of bargaining) or where the appropriate lawmaking body fails to approve a contract reached through collective bargaining, either party may request appointment of an arbitration board. Prior to arbitration, the parties must make every effort including mediation to settle their dispute through good-faith collective bargaining. The mediator's function is to assist all parties in reaching a voluntary agreement, without making any recommendations public.

The written request for arbitration must be initiated within 5 days following the 60-day pre-impasse period. Although voluntary arbitration is encouraged, there is no requirement for compulsory arbitration. If the parties elect arbitration, a written agreement to arbitrate must be signed within 5 days following the request for arbitration. Each party selects one arbitrator, and the two arbitrators select a third neutral arbitrator. A hearing must be held within 10 days, concluded within 20 additional days, and written findings presented within another 10 days. A majority decision of the arbitration board is binding and may be enforced in the district court. Compensation of arbitrators is paid jointly by the parties.

If the public employer refuses arbitration, the district court has jurisdiction to enforce the requirement that compensation and working conditions be based on prevailing wages and conditions in the private sector for jobs requiring similar skill and training. The public employer is liable for court costs, back pay up to one year, and reasonable attorney fees of the employees' association. However, the delegation of authority to the judiciary to fix wages has been found unconstitutional (Op. Atty. Gen. H-965, 1977).

Strikes, lockouts, work stoppages, and slowdowns are prohibited. The district court can fine the employee association the lesser of $20,000 or 1/26 of total annual membership dues, or at least $2,500, for each day of violation. If an employee engages in strikes or picketing, his wages are frozen for one year after return to work. Furthermore, the employee is on probation for two years with respect to civil service or tenure status.

Collective bargaining contracts take precedence over civil service provisions.

The Fire and Police Employee Relations Act does not apply to law enforcement officers employed by a sheriff's department, except those designated as "county police officers" (Op. Atty. Gen. H-918, 1976).

Other Public Employees

All public employees have the right to organize, and they may not be discriminated against because of belonging or not belonging to a union. However, collective bargaining is permitted only to policemen and firemen. The 1947 law prohibits state and local government officials from recognizing a labor organization as bargaining agent for public employees, and from entering into a collective-bargaining contract with a labor organization. Public employees may present grievances concerning wages, hours, and working conditions through a representative of their choosing; but the representative cannot be recognized as a bargaining agent, and cannot be recognized at all if his organization claims the right to strike (R.C.S. Art. 5154c)[1]. The

[1]This right still applies to police and fire employees despite the separate law covering them (Castleberry v. Langford *et al.*, No. CA 3-74-1025-c, 1977).

local union disclaimer of the national union's constitution or bylaws preserving the right to strike would be useless. (Dallas Independent School District v. American Federation of State, County, and Municipal Employees Local 1442, 330 S.W. 2d 702 [Civ. App. 1960]).

Strikes by public employees are outlawed under penalty of forfeiting all civil service rights, reemployment rights, and any other rights or benefits. Membership in a union cannot be cause for denial of employment.

Boards of trustees are now authorized to consult with teachers on matters of educational policy and conditions of employment (R.C.S. Art. 5154c). Teachers have the right to join or not to join professional associations (Texas Education Code Ann. 13.217). Any teacher who goes on strike is suspended from employment (Texas Education Code Ann. 13.216).

Payroll deductions for union dues (check-off) may be authorized in cities of 10,000 or more population and counties of 20,000 or more population. Participation in the program is voluntary and by written request (R.C.S. Art. 6252-3 and 2372h-4).

Regulation of Union Activities

Public policy toward labor unions has shifted through periods of antagonism, encouragement, and, finally, regulation. The Texas Union Regulation Act of 1943, amended in 1975, anticipated many of the provisions of the federal Labor Management Reporting and Disclosure Act of 1959. It covers financial reporting, election procedures, and certain rights of individual union members.

Every labor union required to file reports with the secretary of labor under the federal Labor-Management Reporting and Disclosure Act of 1959 must file a copy of each report with the secretary of state of Texas within 30 days of the date the federal report is filed. (R.C.S. Art. 5154a-3).

All union organizers operating in Texas are required to register with the secretary of state (R.C.S. Art. 5154a-5). This requirement was ruled a valid exercise of the police power of the state in 1945 by the U.S. Court of Civil Appeals (AFL v. Mann, 16 LRRM 634, 188 S.W. 2d 276). However, the U.S. Supreme Court ruled in 1945 that this provision was an unconstitutional violation of the right of free speech when applied to a national union official (Thomas v. Collins, 15 LRRM 777, 323 U.S. 516).

Unions are prohibited from collecting excessive initiation fees, dues, and assessments. They are permitted to collect dues or assessments for purposes which benefit the members, and to maintain funds or make investments for such beneficial programs. Unions may collect dues or assessments for old-age benefits, death and burial benefits; for hospitalization, unemployment, health and accident, retirement, or other forms of mutual insurance; for lobbying, grievance committee, gifts, floral offerings, charitable purposes, strike funds, or any other legitimate practice. The main thrust of the law is against excessive initiation fees, since this could result in severe restriction of union membership (R.C.S. Art. 5154a-7). Labor unions are prohibited from making any financial contribution to any political party or to the campaign expenses of any person running for political office. This does not preclude the use of union funds for such nonpartisan activities as voter registration, worker education, and lobbying. Also, the unions may form separate political funds through voluntary member contributions, which may be used to endorse particular candidates (R.C.S. Art. 5154a).

Union-management contract clauses providing for dues check-off (automatic deduction from pay) must also provide for the written consent of individual employees (R.C.S. Art. 5154e).

Union officials are required to maintain accurate accounts of all receipts and expenditures of union funds, which any member of the union may inspect at all reasonable times (R.C.S. Art. 5154a-9).

Various sections of the Union Regulation Act of 1943 have been held invalid or unconstitutional: an annual financial statement of all union receipts and itemized expenditures, an annual election by secret ballot, and submission of copies of all collective-bargaining agreements to the secretary of state (AFL v. Mann, 16 LRRM 634, 188 S.W. 2d 176).

Other sections on financial reporting and limits on expulsion from a union have been superseded by the Labor Management Reporting and Disclosure Act of 1959.

The Texas Anti-Trust Act forbids combinations to restrain trade, fix prices, lessen competition, or fix output or the amount of work that may be done in preparing a product for sale. It is considered a conspiracy in restraint of trade when any two or more persons or associations agree to refuse to buy or sell to any other persons or groups; to agree to boycott or refuse to transport, receive, use, or work with any products of any other persons.

The provision against handling of goods does not apply to refusal to handle products of the immediate employer, unless this refusal is intended to induce the employer to boycott a third party. For example, the law prohibited the Carpenters' Union from picketing a restaurant whose owner was building a residence at a different location with nonunion labor (Carpenters v. Ritter's Cafe, 6 LRRM 1109, 138 S.W. 2d 828). The Texas Supreme Court has held unconstitutional that part of the Texas Union Regulation Act (R.C.S. Art. 5154f) which restricts the labor dispute to a controversy between an employer and a majority of his employees (International Union of Operating Engineers v. Cox, 23 LRRM 2527, 219 S.W. 2nd 787 [1949]).

Strikes, Picketing, and Secondary Boycotts

The Federal Anti-Injunction (Norris-La Guardia) Act of 1932 restricts the use of injunctions in labor disputes when interstate commerce is involved, and many other states have comparable laws. Texas, however, provides for suits to enjoin unlawful strikes or picketing (R.C.S. 1995-17a).

Strikes

The right to strike is upheld by law, if peaceable and lawful means are used to induce persons to refuse to work. However, one may not trespass on company property without the owner's consent. This right to strike does not apply to any action taken by the union for the purpose of limiting the production, transportation, or consumption of goods. The Texas Supreme Court found it a violation for a union to prevent connecting carriers from handling freight from a carrier not under union contract (Teamsters v. Best Motor Lines, 27 LRRM 2457).

Unions are liable for damages resulting from losses incurred through strikes or picketing by their members if such picketing or strike is held to be breach of contract by the Court (R.C.S. 5154b). Unions can sue and be sued, whether or not they are incorporated, without making the individual members thereof parties to the suit. In such suits service of citation may be had against the president, secretary, or treasurer (R.C.S. Art. 6134); and if judgment is made against the association it becomes binding on the joint property of all members, but not upon their personal property (R.C.S. Art. 6136). If service of citation is issued against a member, execution may be had against the personal property of any member, if the joint property was insufficient to satisfy the claim (R.C.S. Art. 6137).

Strikebreakers

Any person or firm that employs an armed force of detectives or persons not residents of Texas as strikebreakers is liable to pay the state a fine of $25 to $1,000 (R.C.S. Art. 5207).

Picketing

Picketing by a labor union or its members has been legalized with limited objectives of allowing striking employees who have a bona-fide economic dispute with their employer to discourage other employees from entering the place of business. Peaceful picketing is permissible under constitutional provisions guaranteeing the right of speech, but it is also recognized that picketing involves an element of coercion. In Tipton v. Hotel and Restaurant Employees, Local 808, 149 S.W. 2d 1028 (Tex. Civ. App.—Galveston 1941) the Court of Civil Appeals held that "stranger picketing" (by nonemployees) is lawful.

A later act of 1955 forbids picketing of a firm or establishment by a union which does not represent a majority of the employees of the firm or establishment. A trial judge is authorized to order an election to determine whether a union represents a majority. The Labor Management Relations Act of 1947 will supersede where applicable. (R.C.S. Art. 5154g).

A law which prohibits picketing of the plant or property of any public utility (one furnishing electricity, gas, or water to the public) has not been tested, and is probably unconstitutional. Sabotaging of or tampering with utility equipment in order to interfere with service is a felony punishable by two to five years in the state penitentiary (R.C.S. Art. 1446a).

A city ordinance prohibiting picketing on city streets was found valid (*Ex parte* Waltrip, 151 Cr.R. 343, 207 S.W. 2d 872 [1948]). In another case the prohibition of picketing within 100 feet of the spur tracks entering a struck firm was held to abridge the right of free speech.

Five Texas statutes relating to unlawful assembly (P.C. 439), breach of peace (P.C. 474), abusive language (P.C. 482), mass picketing (R.C.S. Art. 5154d) and secondary strikes (R.C.S. Art. 5154f) were found unconstitutional in a case initiated by the United Farm Workers (Allee v. Medrano, 94 S.Ct. 2191, 416 U.S. 802 [1974]). They are replaced by general prohibition against disorderly conduct (P.C. 42.01), riot (P.C. 42.02), obstructing passageways, and disrupting a lawful gathering (P.C. 42.05).

Secondary Boycotts

Secondary strikes, picketing, and boycotts are unlawful in Texas. A secondary strike is a work stoppage where no labor dispute exists between the employer and his employees, and where the work stoppage results from a labor dispute to which such employees are not parties (R.C.S. Art. 5154f). Secondary picketing entails the establishment of pickets at the premises of an employer where no labor dispute exists between such employer and his employees. Secondary boycott includes any agreement or concerted action by two or more persons to cause damage to any firm by which they are not employed by withholding patronage or labor, picketing, refusing to handle goods, forming a strike, attempting to prevent the free flow of commerce, or by any other means causing an employer with whom they have a labor dispute to cause damage to an employer who is not a party to such labor dispute (R.C.S. Art. 5154f).

2

Laws Relating to Wages, Hours, and Working Conditions

Wages

Pay Days

Every private employer (but not the state) must pay his employees at least semimonthly and within 16 days of the day the wages are earned (R.C.S. Art. 5155).

Employees who are absent, laid off, or discharged, or who quit work must be paid in full within six days from termination (R.C.S. Art. 5156).

The Texas Department of Labor and Standards or the attorney general may request the public prosecuting attorney to prosecute an employer for violation of the law. The penalty of $50 for each failure to pay the employee is paid to the state. A new violation occurs for each new day's wages that become overdue. Civil suits for wages in amounts under $200 filed by employees against the employer may be handled in the small claims court.

Employees may file complaints by mail or in person at the nearest field office of the Texas Department of Labor and Standards.

However, the commissioner of labor is not authorized to collect back wages.

Wages on Construction of Public Works (R.C.S. Art. 5159a)

Laborers, workmen, and mechanics employed in the construction and repair of public works for the state of Texas or any of its political subdivisions must be paid not less than the general prevailing rate of pay for similar work in the same locality. This includes workers employed by contractors or subcontractors for public works. The prevailing rate of pay for legal holidays and overtime work will also be paid. The cost of employee fringe benefits may be considered in determining a prevailing wage rate.

The public body awarding a contract specifies in the call for bids and in the contract what the prevailing wage shall be for each craft or type of worker needed. These bid calls and contracts are public documents and may be examined by any workman on the job, at the office of either the public body or the contractor.

If a contractor or subcontractor pays less than the prevailing wage the employee will first request that the wage be paid. If the correction has not been made within six days, he should file a written complaint with an agent of the public body awarding the contract, and report the matter to the nearest district office of the Texas Department of Labor and Standards.

Willful violation of this act, by contractor, subcontractor or public body, is a misdemeanor, punishable by fine of not more than $500 and imprisonment for not more than six months, or both. The contractor forfeits to the public body $10 for each workman for each day of pay less than the prevailing wage. The Davis-Bacon Act provides that the secretary of labor will determine the prevailing wage on contracts funded by the federal government in excess of $2,000.

Scrip

When an employer pays in scrip, coupons, store orders, or any other token form, such scrip will be redeemable in money on demand by the employee (R.C.S. Art. 5159b).

Wage Assignment or Garnishment

An employee cannot assign his unearned wages to any person unless the employer is given written notice immediately after execution of the assignment (R.C.S. Art. 5159c).

The Texas Constitution provides that current wages for personal service cannot be subject to garnishment (Art. 16, Sec. 28). This supersedes Section 303(a) of the Federal Consumer Credit Protection Act of 1968, which permits garnishment of a maximum of 25% of an individual's weekly disposable earnings.

An employer cannot make any other wage deductions without the employee's consent, except for FITW and FICA. Reasonable provisions may be made for pay deductions to cover losses caused by an employee's negligence or incompetence.

Bond to Secure Wages

Contractor's bond for performance and payment for labor and materials is required on all public contracts. After completion and acceptance of the project all moneys due the contractor are held by the public agency until evidence is submitted by the contractor that all bills for labor and material have been paid in full. All claims for payments must be itemized and sworn to as required for mechanic's-lien claims, and filed with the county clerk within 90 days from delivery of material or performance of work (R.C.S. Art. 5160). If the bond is inadequate to pay all claims, judgment is given to each creditor pro rata of the amount of the recovery on the bond (R.C.S. Art. 5163).

Mechanic's Liens

The law provides that workers shall have a lien on the buildings and articles made by them for the value of their labor or materials furnished (Tex. Const. Art. XVI, Sec. 37; R.C.S. Arts. 5352-5472). The lien must be filed within three months of the indebtedness (R.C.S. Art. 5453).

Farm, factory, office, and store employees may fix a lien against the business assets of the employer. It must be filed within 30 days, and is effective for 6 months (R.C.S. Art. 5483). For the purpose of a lien all wages are due weekly in lawful money for work performed by day or week (R.C.S. Art. 5485). Whenever an employer refuses to make payment the employee should prepare a statement in duplicate of the amount due, present one copy to the employer, and file another copy with the county clerk in the county where the work was performed. The lien is effective for six months, unless suit is brought to enforce the lien (R.C.S. Art. 5486).

Equal Pay

Women employed by the state must be paid at the same rate as men for the same kind, grade, and quantity of services (R.C.S. Arts. 4594-4595). Federal law extends the same requirements to private employment. (See "Fair Employment Practices.")

Minimum Wages and Overtime

The Federal Fair Labor Standards Act of 1938, as amended to 1977, establishes a minimum wage and overtime pay for work over 40 hours a week. At first this federal law was limited to employees who worked directly in interstate commerce, but several amendments have gradually extended the coverage to most workers except in certain smaller enterprises. The Texas Minimum Wage Act became effective February 1, 1970. It covers many employees who are exempt from the federal law. Employees who are not covered under either law are chiefly those in small establishments, amusement enterprises, and government employment. Agricultural workers are covered separately in both federal and state law.

Federal Fair Labor Standards Act (FLSA)

The Fair Labor Standards Act of 1938, as amended to 1977, requires payment of a minimum hourly wage according to the following schedule:

$2.65 effective January 1, 1978
2.90 effective January 1, 1979
3.10 effective January 1, 1980
3.35 effective January 1, 1981

One and one-half times the employee's regular pay rate for all hours worked in excess of 40 per week is also required.

Coverage. Prior to 1967 the Act covered employees in interstate or foreign commerce. The amendments of 1967, 1972, and 1974 added coverage of most other private and public employment.

Covered employees include workers in these categories: (1) employees individually engaged in interstate or foreign commerce in transportation, communication, and distribution; employees of banks and insurance companies that utilize interstate commerce; and employees who travel across state lines while working; (2) employees individually engaged in production of goods for interstate commerce—those who work in establishments which produce goods for interstate commerce, or in an industry essential to production of such goods; (3) all employees in retail or service establishments grossing at least $250,000 annually ($275,000 in sales effective July 1, 1978, $325,000 on July 1, 1980, and $362,500 on December 31, 1981); (4) construction (regardless of dollar volume); (5) laundry or dry cleaning (regardless of dollar volume); (6) hospitals and nursing homes, schools and colleges; (7) federal, state, local and interstate governments and agencies;[1] (8) domestic service workers if they receive at least $50 in cash wages in a calendar quarter from their employer, or work more than eight hours a week for one or more employers; and (9) workers employed in agriculture by an employer who used more than 500 man-days of farm labor in any calendar quarter of the preceding calendar year.[2]

---

[1]The U.S. Supreme Court has ruled that the minimum wage and overtime provisions of the FLSA are not applicable to the integral operations of the states and their political subdivisions in areas of traditional government functions. Such areas include schools and hospitals, fire prevention, police protection, sanitation, public health, and parks and recreation (National League of Cities v. Usery, U.S. 96 S.C. 2465, 49 L.Ed. 2d 245, 1976).

[2]A Texas farm corporation was found in violation of the FLSA for employing child labor and paying less than the federal minimum wage. It was held that, although the field workers were supplied and paid through crew leaders, the corporation was directly responsible for compliance with the law. The company had contended that the crew leaders were independent contractors (James D. Hodgson, Secretary of Labor, United States Department of Labor, v. Griffin and Brand of McAllan, Incorporated, U.S. District Civil Action No. 70-B-65 filed March 31, 1972).

Exemptions. Remaining exemptions from the federal minimum-wage and overtime provisions include: (1) executive, administrative, and professional employees; (2) employees of a retail or service establishment that makes more than 50% of its sales within the state and is not a covered enterprise (as listed above); (3) employees of seasonal amusement or recreational establishments, movie theaters, small newspapers, small telephone companies, seamen employed on foreign vessels; fishermen; farm workers employed by a farmer who did not use more than 500 man-days of farm labor in any calendar quarter; employees of companies dealing with specific agricultural or horticultural commodities; workers in small forestry operations; (4) casual babysitters and companions to the elderly; and (5) outside salesworkers.

Exemption from only the overtime requirements applies to broadcasting employees in towns of less than 100,000 population; auto salesworkers; local deliverymen paid on the basis of trip rates; taxicab drivers; farm truckers; live-in domestic workers; employees of livestock auctions, country elevators, and maple sugar processing.

Tips, Meals, and Lodging. The minimum wage may include the amount of tips as determined by the employer, but tips cannot comprise more than 50% of the minimum-wage rate (55% in 1979, and 60% in 1980). Meals and lodging at actual cost furnished to an employee may be included in computing the minimum wage, if their cost is stated separately on the employee's earnings statement.

Overtime. Special overtime provisions apply in certain cases. A workweek longer than 40 hours may be established under FLSA in the following instances:

1. A collective bargaining agreement provides that an employee during a 52-week period works no longer than 2240 hours and is guaranteed from 1840 to 2080 hours; however, overtime rates apply above this.
2. Employees of an independent local petroleum distributor if the annual sales volume is less than $1 million, more than 75% of sales is made intrastate, and no more than 25% of sales is to customers who are engaged in bulk distribution of such

products for resale; however, overtime rates apply after 12 hours in any workday or 56 hours in any workweek.

3. Employees of retail or service establishments whose regular rate of pay is in excess of one and one-half times the minimum wage, and more than one-half of the compensation represents commissions.
4. Hospital employees who agree to a work period of 14 consecutive days in lieu of 7 consecutive days for purposes of overtime computation; then overtime pay begins after 8 hours in any workday and 80 hours in a 14-day period.
5. Fire protection employees are subject to overtime pay when work time exceeds 216 hours in a work period of 28 days.
6. Seasonal workers (not more than 14 weeks in any calendar year) in the tobacco industry; however, overtime pay is required for work in excess of 10 hours per day or 48 hours per week.
7. Hotel employees other than maids or custodians, who are paid one and one-half times the regular rate for work over 44 hours per week. (This drops to 40 hours after January 1, 1979).
8. Cotton gin or sugar processing employees who are paid time and one-half for employment in excess of 60 hours a week for up to 6 weeks a year, 56 hours a week for up to 4 weeks a year, 48 hours a week for up to 2 weeks a year, and 44 hours for any other workweek in that year.

Students and Handicapped Workers. Employers may hire up to four full-time students at 85% of the minimum wage by filing an application with the secretary of labor. Employment of more than four students at this rate must receive prior certification from the secretary of labor. The proportion of student hours under certification cannot exceed the proportion of student hours of the preceding year, or 10% of all hours, whichever is greater. Colleges and universities may employ their full-time students for up to 20 hours per week at 85% of the minimum wage with no restrictions on numbers.

Handicapped workers may be hired under special certificates at wages not less than 50% of the minimum wage.

Texas Minimum Wage Act

The Texas Minimum Wage Act of 1970 provides that every employer must pay each employee at least $1.40 an hour after

February 1, 1971. Exemptions are indicated below (R.C.S. Art. 5159d-5).

Employees in Agriculture. The state minimum wage for agricultural employees is $0.20 less than the federal minimum wage for agriculture (as provided in Fair Labor Standards Act of 1938, as amended) and not more than the minimum rate for other workers in Texas. Since the federal minimum agricultural wage is $2.65, the state minimum rate of $1.40 per hour applies; for workers living on premises provided by the employer the minimum weekly salary is $30, in addition to the living quarters. A member of the employee's family living in the quarters may be employed at less than this wage without regard to the minimum-wage provisions (R.C.S. Art. 5159d-6).

Piece-rate Workers (Hand Harvesters). The commissioner of agriculture determines a piece rate for each agricultural commodity commercially produced in substantial quantity in Texas, based on the output of a worker of average ability which would equal the minimum wage (that is, if the commissioner determines the average worker picks ten gallons of berries an hour, the piece rate will be set at $0.14 a gallon, to provide $1.40 an hour). The piece rate, not the hourly rate, will be the legal minimum. If no piece rate is set the minimum hourly rate for agricultural workers will apply (R.C.S. Art. 5159d-7).

Exemptions from the Texas State Law. Several categories of employers are exempt from the requirements of the Texas law (R.C.S. Art. 5159d-4).

1. *Those covered by the Fair Labor Standards Act.* Any employer covered by provisions of the federal Fair Labor Standards Act of 1938, as amended, is exempt from the state law.
2. *Those employing fewer than a specified number.* Agricultural employers are exempt from the state minimum-wage law if they used fewer than 300 man-days (one man-day = four hours) of agricultural labor in any calendar quarter during the preceding calendar year. All other employers are exempt if they are exempt from the Texas Unemployment Compensation Act.

3. *Those in the livestock and dairy industries.* Employers engaged in the production of livestock or in dairy farming are excluded from this law.
4. *Other exemptions.* Employers are exempt from the state minimum-wage law with respect to employment of the following: (1) members of a religious order; (2) persons under eighteen not a high-school or vocational-school graduate, persons under twenty enrolled in any school (does not apply to agricultural piece-rate workers); (3) executive, administrative, or professional workers; (4) outside salesmen on a commission basis; (5) switchboard operators of independent telephone companies with fewer than 750 stations; (6) domestic servants in a private home; (7) prison laborers; (8) workers in nonprofit organizations where the services are performed by unpaid volunteers, or where the employer-employee relationship does not exist; (9) certain relatives; (10) handicapped persons under twenty-one participating in a work-school program of vocational education; (11) employees of an amusement establishment if it operates less than seven months a year, or if its receipts for any six months in a year were less than one-third of receipts for the other six months; (12) employees of the Boy Scouts and Girl Scouts of America; (13) camps operated by nonprofit organizations; and (14) employees of nonprofit educational institutions who serve as foster parents in their own home, or receive room and board in the institution.
5. *Disabled workers.* Persons whose productive capacity is impaired by disability or who are over 65 years of age may be employed at less than the minimum wage, but not less than 60%. This does not apply to piece-rate workers in agriculture. The disability must be verified by a medical certificate signed by a licensed physician (R.C.S. Art. 5159d-9).
6. *Sheltered workshop.* Nonprofit organizations, such as Goodwill Industries, which train and employ the handicapped under federal regulation are exempt (R.C.S. Art. 5159d-10).

Employer's Statement. The employer must provide a written and signed earnings statement with each pay check. The statement must include name of the employee, rate of pay, total amount earned during pay period, any deductions made from pay, net pay, total number of hours (or amount of work done if paid on a piece basis). A notation on the statement, "medical certificate" or "agriculture" must appear where applicable (R.C.S. Art. 5159d-11).

Penalties. Furnishing a false earnings statement for the purpose of depriving an employee of minimum wages is a misdemeanor punishable by a fine of $100-$500 and/or by confinement in the county jail for 5 to 30 days. An employer who pays less than the appropriate minimum wage is liable to the employees affected in the amount of the unpaid wages plus an additional equal amount as liquidated damages, plus attorney's fee and court costs (R.C.S. Art. 5159d-12, 13). No provision has been made for enforcement of the law, and employees must go to court to collect unpaid wages.

Voting Time

An employee is entitled to time off for voting if he does not have sufficient time for voting otherwise. Such time off may not be deducted from the employee's wages (Op. Atty. Gen. No. V-1475, 1952). The employer may designate the time of day allotted for voting (Op. Atty. Gen. No. 0-6242, 1944 and Texas Election Code, Art. 15.14). This does not require payment for loss of voluntary overtime work and pay (Op. Atty. Gen. No. M-53, 1967).

Child Labor

A child in Texas is a person under the age of 18. Married persons regardless of age have adult status.

Federal Law

The Fair Labor Standards Act prohibits "oppressive child labor" in industries engaged in interstate or foreign commerce. The minimum legal age for employment is

1. Fourteen years for occupations other than manufacturing and mining which will not interfere with schooling, health, and well-being.
2. Sixteen years for most employment covered by the act.

3. Eighteen years for employment in a nonagricultural occupation declared hazardous by the secretary of labor.

Exemptions from Federal Child Labor Laws

1. Children under the age of 12 may be employed outside of school hours on a farm owned or operated by a parent, or on another farm exempt from the minimum wage law, with parent's approval.
2. Children 12 or 13 years of age may be employed in agriculture outside of school hours with consent of parent.
3. Children 14 years of age or older may be employed in agriculture outside of school hours.
4. Children under the age of 16 may not be employed in agriculture in a hazardous occupation except by the parent.
5. Child labor as an actor, in the delivery of newspapers, or in making evergreen wreaths, is exempt.
6. Children 14 and 15 years old may not be employed before 7 a.m. or after 7 p.m. (after 9 p.m. from June 1 through Labor Day); more than 3 hours a day or 18 hours a week in school periods; more than 8 hours a day or 40 hours a week in non-school periods.

State Law (R.C.S. Art. 5181)

Employment of children under the age of 15 is prohibited in any factory, mill, workshop, or laundry; in messenger service in towns of more than 15,000 population; and wherever dangerous machinery is used (R.C.S. Art. 5181a). Children under 15 may not work over 8 hours a day, over 48 hours a week, or between 10 p.m. and 5 a.m. (R.C.S. Art. 5181d).

Employment of minors under 17 is prohibited in any mine, quarry, or place where explosives are used (R.C.S. Art. 5181b). Minors under 17 may not be sent to any disorderly house or other place of amusement conducted for immoral purposes, the character or reputation of which could have been determined on reasonable inquiry by the employer (R.C.S. Art. 5181b and c).

Children of any age may be employed as nurse, maid, gardener, or in another job for private households; or at farm labor as members of the family on their own premises (R.C.S. Art. 5181g). Children of any age may work between June 1 and September 1, except where employment of children is prohibited above.

A special permit should be obtained from the county judge to permit the employment of a child over the age of 14 whose earnings are necessary for the support of the child or the members of the child's family. The child or his parents or guardian must furnish an affidavit that the child is over 14 years of age, has completed the seventh grade in school, and will not be employed in any place or condition prohibited to children under 17; that the earnings are necessary for family support; and that suitable employment has been obtained. A medical certificate must be furnished showing the child is physically able to perform the work. The child and the parent or guardian must appear in person before the judge to request the permit. (R.C.S. Art. 5181e). The permit must be posted in a public place by the employer, and must be renewed every 12 months.

The commissioner of labor and standards or any of his deputies or inspectors must have free access during working hours to all places where minors are employed (R.C.S. 5181f).

Parents or guardians, as well as employers, who permit violation of the law are subject to fines and imprisonment (R.C.S. Art. 5181h).

Employment Agencies

Private Employment Agencies (R.C.S. Art. 5221a)

All private employment agencies must be licensed by the state. Executive search firms, résumé services, and overseas placement services are subject to the Act. The exceptions to the law are persons who charge a fee of $2 or less for employment registration of public school teachers and administrators; government agencies; agencies operated for the purpose of employing help for one's own business; farmers or stock-raisers acting jointly or severally in obtaining labor for their own use where no placement fee is charged; charitable associations chartered under state law for the purpose of conducting a free employment agency; family members acting for each other; veterans' associations; labor unions; nurses' registry operated and conducted by registered nurses; a labor agency; and part-time or temporary-help businesses.

Operators of employment agencies must apply for a license and pass an examination covering the laws and regulations relating to the operation of a private employment agency, laws relating to discrimination in employment, other labor laws, and general matters relating to operation of agencies of employment. An operator applicant must be a U.S. citizen and a resident of Texas for at least the immediately previous year, must possess good moral character, and must never have been convicted of an offense involving moral turpitude. A private employment agency license can be issued only to a licensed operator. Each applicant for a private employment agency license or renewal thereof must make and file a bond of $5,000. Licenses are renewed annually on August 31.

Employment agencies licensed by the state are not permitted to:

1. Charge any fee for the registration of employment applicants, except for furnishing of employment obtained directly through the efforts of the agency;
2. Split or attempt to split fees with an employer or his agent;
3. Charge a fee greater than authorized by the Texas Private Employment Agency Regulatory Board;
4. Make any false promise or misrepresentation;
5. Refer any applicant to a place where a strike or lockout exists without furnishing a written statement as to the existence of such strike or lockout;
6. Procure or attempt to procure a person's discharge from employment, or influence an employee to quit his job;
7. Use any name, sign, or advertising device similar or reasonably confused with the name of a government agency, or which is false or misleading to the private agency;
8. Refer any applicant to a job without a valid job order, to an employment prohibited by law, or to an employment deleterious to health or morals;
9. Violate any state or federal law;
10. Require job applicants to subscribe to any publication or incidental service.

The Texas Private Employment Agency Regulatory Board has authority to regulate private employment agencies in the State, and to direct the Texas Department of Labor and Standards in this area. The board is composed of nine members appointed by the governor, all of whom must have been actively engaged as operators of private employment agencies for a minimum period of five years.

The Texas Department of Labor and Standards is assigned to enforce and administer the act and the rules and regulations of the board, through inspection of the agency and the records of the agency, and where necessary after due process seek injunctive relief. The board has subpoena and license revokation authorities.

The board has established the following maximum fee schedule:

4% of agreed annual gross earnings through $4,999 (or 48% of the first month's stated salary)
5% from $5,000 through $5,999
6% from $6,000 through $6,999
7% from $7,000 through $7,999
$8,000 and above may be by individual contract between the applicant and the agency

The maximum fee for temporary employment is 20% of gross earnings. This applies when termination for good cause occurs within the first 30 days of employment. Good cause is defined as any of the following:

1. Wages, salary, working hours, working days, working shift, type of work assigned and geographical location of the job are significantly different from the terms agreed upon. Exception: an applicant hired as a "trainee" agrees that the choice of actual assignment remains with the employer.
2. Lack of applicant's job skills or physical ability to perform the duties of the job agreed upon (provided applicant is not in violation of section 3b pre-employment misrepresentation).
3. The job is eliminated because of lockout, strike, lay-off, or employer reduction in work force.
4. Physical or economic destruction of the business.
5. Applicant's entry into the military service.
6. Death of the applicant.
7. Immoral or illegal activities on the part of the employer.

Labor Agents

The Labor Agency Law (R.C.S. Art. 5221a-5) applies to any person in Texas who obtains or attempts to obtain employment for common laborers or agricultural workers to work in Texas or outside of Texas. Most of those exceptions to the Private Employment Agency Law also apply to the Labor Agency Law, with the Labor Agency Law applying to common laborers and agricultural workers and the Private Employment Agency Law affecting the placement of all other workers.

Labor agents must be licensed by the state, upon application accompanied by affidavits of at least five creditable citizens who have resided in the county for at least three years to the effect that the applicant is of good moral character. The license costs $150 for each county in which the labor agent will operate. He must also furnish $5,000 bond. If the labor agent solicits workers to be employed outside the state he must pay an annual state occupation tax of $600, and a county occupation tax of $100-$300 according to county size.

Most of the prohibitions to private employment agencies are also prohibited to labor agents under the Labor Agency Law. In addition, a labor agent cannot charge more than $3.00 for securing employment for a common laborer or farm worker. A labor agent must also report monthly to the Texas Department of Labor and Standards information identifying workers, employers, the kind, location, and length of the work, the wages to be paid, and the mode of arrangements for the transportation of the workers.

Fair Employment Practices

Federal Laws

Federal laws and executive orders prohibiting discrimination in employment are applicable to most employers in the state.

Title VII of the Civil Rights Act of 1964, as amended to 1972, forbids employment discrimination because of race, color, religion, sex, and national origin. The law is enforced by the Equal Employment Opportunity Commission. It applies to employers engaged in an industry affecting interstate commerce who have at least fifteen employees. Governmental agencies, labor unions, educational institutions, employment agencies, and joint apprenticeship programs are also included. Private clubs and Indian reservations are exempt. Title VII also allows exceptions where religion, sex, or national origin is a bona fide occupational qualification.

The Age Discrimination in Employment Act of 1967 prohibits discrimination on the basis of age against persons who are between 40 and 65 years old. The law applies to employers of 25 or more workers for each working day in 20 or more calendar weeks in a year, in an industry affecting commerce; labor unions maintaining a hiring hall or having 25 or more members; and all employment agencies. The term "employer" does not include the United States, a corporation wholly owned by the U.S. government, or a state or political subdivision thereof. The act also allows exceptions based on bona fide occupational qualifications.

The Equal Pay Act of 1972 requires equal pay for men and women performing equal work. It applies to employers covered under the minimum wage provisions of the Fair Labor Standards Act of 1938.

Executive Order 11246 prohibits discrimination by government contractors and subcontractors on the basis of race, color, religion, and national origin. Executive Order 11141 prohibits age discrimination. Executive Order 11478 bans sex discrimination against federal employees. The Office of Federal Contract Compliance in the Department of Labor was created to enforce E.O. 11246. The General Services Administration enforces E.O. 11141. The Civil Service Commission provides guidance in compliance with E.O. 11478. There are no exemptions from the executive orders.

Title VII invalidates state laws which are inconsistent with federal law. Compliance with state laws will not excuse noncompliance with the Equal Pay Act, nor will compliance with the Equal Pay Act excuse noncompliance with state laws with higher standards.

State Laws

A Texas law of 1963 discourages age discrimination in public employment by prohibiting any public agency from setting a minimum age over 21 or a maximum age under 65, thus guaranteeing freedom from discrimination for persons between these ages. This law does not apply to firemen, law-enforcement officers, or colleges with established retirement programs (R.C.S. Art. 6252-14).

A 1967 law prohibits job discrimination in employment by the state or its political subdivisions because of race, religion, color, or national origin. This prohibition on discriminatory action applies to employment, issuance of licenses or permits, use of public facilities, programs, benefits, and bids. A civil action for preventive relief may be instituted through the district attorney and/or county attorney (R.C.S. Art. 6252-16).

Article 1, Section 3a, of the Texas Constitution was amended in 1972 to state that equality under the law shall not be denied or abridged because of sex, race, color, creed, or national origin.

An employer may not discriminate against a handicapped person if the person is qualified for the job (R.C.S. Art. 4419e-3).

Jury Duty

A permanent employee may not be terminated because of absence for jury duty (R.C.S. Art. 5207b).

Employment of Aliens

The Immigration and Nationality Act regulates the admission of aliens into the United States. The department of labor issues labor certifications for both the temporary and permanent employment of aliens in the United States. For permanent employment, the United States Employment Service has determined that there are not enough U.S. workers available, and that wages and working conditions of U.S. workers will not be adversely affected by the employment of aliens, in the occupations listed in Schedule A. The U.S.E.S. has determined that U.S. workers would be adversely affected by employment of aliens in Schedule B occupation.

Schedule A. (1) M.A.'s and Ph.D.'s in dietetics, bachelor's degrees in physical therapy; (2) aliens of exceptional ability in the sciences or arts (not performing arts) including college and university teachers of exceptional ability; (3) religious preachers and teachers; (4) executives of international organizations or corporations.

Schedule B. A list of 49 occupations requiring little education or experience, such as attendants, bartenders, cashiers, clerks, cooks, domestics, janitors, key punch operators, laborers, nurses aides, telephone operators, truck drivers, yard workers.

3 Unemployment Insurance

Unemployment compensation was inaugurated as a depression measure when a system of national unemployment insurance was made a part of the Social Security Act of 1935. The purpose of the law is to provide minimum income and sustain purchasing power during periods of temporary unemployment. It will keep the worker off welfare and keep total spending from declining rapidly. The federal law was set up so that state legislation meeting certain federal criteria could waive 90% of the federal tax. All states complied quickly, but aside from the minimum standards set by federal law, there is a wide variety of benefits, contributions, coverage, and qualification. For example, maximum weekly unemployment compensation rates range from $80 in Mississippi to $174 in Connecticut.

The Texas Unemployment Compensation Act of 1936, as amended to 1977, provides benefits to qualified unemployed workers at the rate of $15 to $84 per full week of total unemployment, for a maximum of 26 to 39 weeks. Payments are financed by employer contributions based on experience ratings.

Covered Employment

Employers

An employing unit is a subject employer, and its workers are covered under the program if in the current or preceding calendar year, any of the following apply:

1. It paid as much as $1,500 in wages in any calendar quarter or employed at least one individual in each of 20 different calendar weeks.
2. It acquired the business of a subject employer.
3. It is a nonprofit organization exempt from federal income tax and employs 4 or more individuals for 20 calendar weeks. (Churches and organizations operated primarily for religious purposes are excluded.)
4. It is subject to the Federal Unemployment Tax Act and has any employees in Texas.
5. It has elected to become a subject employer.
6. It is a state or political subdivision thereof or any instrumentality which is wholly owned by the state or its political subdivisions.
7. It paid as much as $20,000 in wages to agricultural labor during any calendar quarter, or employed at least 10 workers for at least 20 calendar weeks. Crew leaders are considered employers under specific conditions. This does not apply to legal alien farm labor until January 1, 1980.
8. It paid as much as $1,000 in a calendar quarter to domestic servants in a private home, local college club or local chapter of a college sorority or fraternity.

Employees

An unemployed individual who meets the following criteria is eligible to receive benefits:

1. He was employed by a firm subject to the act.
2. He has received benefit wage credits of at least $500 within his base period (four consecutive calendar quarters out of the five calendar quarters preceding his benefit period); and he has total benefit wage credits in his base period of at least one and one-half times his highest quarter benefit wage credits.
3. He has registered for work at an employment office, and has claimed benefits.
4. He is able to work, and available for work. (However, he may receive benefits while in a training program approved by the commission.)

5. He has had a waiting period of seven days of unemployment. (After he receives in benefits equal to three times his weekly benefit amount, he is eligible to receive back benefits for the first week.)

Benefits

For each week of total unemployment, each eligible individual receives 1/25 of his or her earnings in the highest benefit quarter. On claims filed on or after October 1, 1977, the maximum weekly benefit rate is $84 and the minimum is $15. Weekly benefit amounts will increase with the statewide level of earnings. For each $10 increase over the previous calendar year in the average weekly wages of production workers in manufacturing in Texas, the maximum and minimum weekly benefit amount will increase by $7 and $1, respectively. The increase becomes effective annually on valid initial claims filed on or after October 1 following publication of the Texas Employment Commission's *Average Weekly Wages Report.*

For weeks of partial unemployment each eligible individual receives the benefit amount plus 25% or $5.00, whichever is greater, less his earnings.

The duration of benefits is limited to 26 times the benefit amount, or 27% of wages during the base period, whichever is less. This ordinarily amounts to 26 weeks of maximum benefits, unless the worker has been unemployed from time to time during the base period, and so has earned less wages.

Employees of educational institutions are not eligible for unemployment compensation during established vacation periods or holiday recess or between academic terms, if there is a contract or reasonable assurance of re-employment when school begins again. This applies to instructional, research, and principal administrative employees in institutions of higher education; and to all employees in other educational institutions.

Benefits cannot be paid to athletes whose services consist of participation in sports or athletic events, for any week between two successive sport seasons if the individual performed the services in the first season and there is reasonable assurance that the individual will perform the services in the following season.

Benefits cannot be paid on the basis of services performed by illegal aliens.

Benefits cannot be denied to an individual solely on the basis of pregnancy or termination of pregnancy.

Benefit wage credits for newly covered employees (agriculture, domestic service, government, schools) shall include wages for previously uncovered service when reimbursable from the federal government.

Computation of Benefit Amount and Duration of Benefits

Step 1. *Determine base period:* It is the first four of the last five completed calendar quarters immediately preceding the quarter in which is filed an initial claim establishing a benefit year.

Base Period					
1st Quarter 1977	2nd Quarter 1977	3rd Quarter 1977	4th Quarter 1977	1st Quarter 1978	Initial Claim
$1,950	$1,750	$2,000	$1,500	$1,500	April 15, 1978

Step 2. *Determine benefit amount for total unemployment:* Take 1/25 of highest quarterly earnings in base period. $2000 ÷ 25 = $80 = benefit amount (benefits payable for each benefit period of 7 days of total unemployment).

Step 3. *Determine maximum benefits payable during benefit year:* Take the lesser of 26 times benefit amount or 27% of total wage credits in base period. 26 x $80 = $2,080.

$1,950	
1,750	Base Period Wage Credits
2,000	
1,500	
$7,200	

27% of $7,200 = $1,944

$1,944 is therefore maximum benefits payable.

Step 4. *Determine maximum number of benefit periods of total unemployment for which benefits may be paid:* Divide benefit amount into the maximum benefits payable. $1,944 ÷ $80 = 24 benefit periods of total unemployment payable during benefit year.

Computation of Benefits for Partial Unemployment

Benefit amount	$80.00
Earnings in benefit period	$50.00

$ 80.00	Benefit amount
20.00	Amount added under provisions of subsection 3(c) ($5.00 or 25% of benefit amount, whichever is greater)
$100.00	Total
50.00	Deduct earnings
$ 50.00	Amount payable

Extended Benefits

Claimants who have exhausted benefits may receive extended benefits when the national rate of insured unemployment (seasonally adjusted) rises to 4.5% or more for 3 months, until the rate has dropped below 4.5% for 3 consecutive months. Extended benefits also begin when for 3 months the rate of insured unemployment (not seasonally adjusted) in Texas equals or exceeds 120% of the corresponding 13-week period in the 2 preceding calendar years, or equals at least 4%. Extended benefits are no longer applicable when the state insured unemployment rate falls below 5%.

Extended benefits are set at the weekly amount payable during the benefit year, for a period up to 50% of the total number of benefit weeks available.

Disqualifications

An individual is disqualified for benefits, or penalized for a certain number of weeks (as determined by the Texas Employment Commission according to the circumstances in each case) for the following causes:

1. A voluntary resignation may be cause for disqualification for any period up to 25 weeks.
2. A discharge for misconduct may be cause for disqualification up to 26 weeks.
3. Failure to apply for, or accept, suitable work may result in disqualification for up to 13 weeks. ("Suitable work" takes into account the risk of the job, physical fitness, prior training, experience and prior earnings, length of unemployment and the employee's prospects for returning to his customary job, and distance of the job from his residence.) An individual may, however, refuse without penalty otherwise suitable work if the position is vacant because of a labor dispute, if substantially less than the prevailing wage is offered, or if the applicant would be required to join or resign from any labor union.
4. An individual is disqualified entirely when unemployment is due to a strike or lockout at his place of work, or at another plant of the same employer which supplies material or services to his place of work. This disqualification does not apply if he is not directly interested in the labor dispute and if he does not belong to a class of workers any of whom are participating in the labor dispute. Neither is he disqualified if he can show that he is not a member of the labor union involved and that he has made an unconditional offer to return to work at the place where he was last employed.
5. An individual is disqualified from receiving benefits for any benefit week in which he received wages in lieu of notice, vacation pay, disability compensation under Workmen's Compensation Law, or Old Age Benefits under the Social Security Act. However, if such benefit is less than unemployment compensation, claimant is entitled to the difference. Severance pay based on prior service does not disqualify the employee, nor does the Supplemental Unemployment Benefit payment provided in auto-union contracts.
6. Students are disqualified for any period of unemployment when the individual has left his most recent full-time work to attend school, unless in training approved by the commission.
7. An individual is disqualified from receiving benefits for weeks

of unemployment after March 1, 1980, for any benefit period for which the individual is receiving a governmental or other pension, retirement pay, annuity, or any other similar periodic payment based on previous work. However, if such pay is less than the unemployment compensation, claimant is entitled to the difference.

The weeks of disqualification under 1, 2, and 3 are deducted from the number of benefit periods of eligibility.

Contributions

Each employer's tax rate is 2.7% (plus 0.5-0.7% federal tax) of the first $6,000 wages paid to each employee until he becomes eligible for an experience tax rate, which is based on benefits paid to former employee claimants.

An employer is eligible for an experience tax rate as soon as his account has been chargeable with benefits throughout four consecutive calendar quarters.

If an employer acquires all or part of the business of another employer, they may make a joint application for total or partial transfer of the compensation experience to the succeeding employer. If only a part of the business is acquired, it must be shown that it is a part to which a definitely identifiable and segregable part of the predecessor's compensation experience was and is attributable.

Annual experience tax rates are computed as of October 1 to be effective for the following calendar year, and notices of the rates are mailed to employers each January.

An employer's experience tax rate is determined by multiplying his benefit ratio by the statewide replenishment ratio for the preceding year.

An employer's benefit ratio is the result obtained by dividing the total benefits paid to his former employees and charged to his account during the preceding 36 months by the employer's total taxable payroll on which taxes have been paid for the same 36 months. If the employer has less than 36 months but at least 4 calendar quarters throughout which his account has been chargeable with benefits, his computation will be based on all calendar quarters immediately preceding the computation date.

The replenishment ratio for a calendar year is obtained by dividing "benefits" by "chargebacks" of the preceding year. The "benefits" are the amount of benefits paid from the Unemployment Compensation Fund during the 12 months ending September 30 of the preceding year, less benefit warrants cancelled, repayment of benefits overpaid, and benefits repayable from reimbursing employers, the federal government, or any other government body. "Chargebacks" are the total amount of chargebacks to the accounts of all taxed employers during that year.

Following is an example of the computation of an employer's experience tax rate:

Total amount of benefits paid to former employees of a taxed employer and charged to his account for the period from October 1, 1976 through September 30, 1977 = $400

Total taxable wages paid by an employer during above period on which the tax was paid = $40,000

The employer's benefit ratio is, therefore, $400 ÷ $40,000 = 1.00%

Assume that the statewide replenishment ratio for Texas for 1978 tax rates = 1.30

Then the employer's 1978 computed experience tax rate will be 1.00% x 1.30 = 1.30%

Section 7 of the Texas Unemployment Compensation Act contains a table showing the various computed experience tax rates depending upon the replenishment ratios and the employer's benefit ratio.

The act also provides for a statewide tax reduction or increase depending upon the amount in the Unemployment Compensation Fund on October 1 of the preceding year. For example, if on October 1, 1977, the amount in the fund exceeded $325 million, a statewide reduction of experience tax rates for 1978 would be applicable. The amount of the reduction would be determined by the amount in the fund.

A rate reduction under this provision of the law may not exceed 2.2%. Regardless of the fund balance adjustment, however, no employer's effective tax rate can be less than 0.1%. No effective tax rate may exceed 4.0% unless the amount in the trust fund is below $225,000,000 as of an October 1 computation date for experience tax rates.

Contributions for Government Employees

A state or its political subdivision or its instrumentality may elect to pay reimbursements for benefits paid in lieu of tax contributions. Each reimbursing employer pays quarterly an amount equal to the regular benefit plus 50% of the extended benefits, (100% beginning January 1, 1979).

Beginning in 1978, each governmental employer electing the tax system must pay 1% of wages during each quarter in 1978 and 1979. In 1980 the contribution rate will be determined by the ratio of benefits paid to wages paid for the preceding two calendar years.

Exemptions

Employment in the following categories is excluded from provisions of the Texas Unemployment Compensation Act unless the employer waives exclusion:

1. Services covered under the Railroad Retirement Act
2. Agricultural labor, when employer is not covered
3. Domestic service performed in a college, club, or private home, when employer is not covered
4. Service of a minor child in the employ of his father or mother
5. Service of an individual in the employ of his son, daughter, or spouse
6. Service performed in the employ of a church or organization operated primarily for religious purposes
7. Service performed in the employ of a political subdivision of the state by elected officials, members of a legislative body, members of the judiciary, emergency crews, or temporary consultants
8. Service performed in the employ of a foreign government or instrumentality of a foreign government if that government grants same exemption to U.S.
9. Service performed as a student nurse or an intern in the employ of a hospital
10. Service performed as an insurance agent or solicitor if remuneration is solely by way of commission
11. Service of newsboys under the age of 18

12. Service performed in the employ of the U.S. government
13. Service performed by an ordained minister in the exercise of his ministry or by a member of a religious order in the exercise of duties required by such order
14. Service performed by members of a fishing crew of ten or fewer workers who are paid on a share basis
15. Service performed by an individual receiving rehabilitation work in a facility conducted for the purpose of carrying out a program of rehabilitation of the handicapped
16. Service performed as part of an unemployment work relief or work training program assisted or financed by a federal or state agency
17. Service performed by an inmate of a custodial or penal institution operated by the state or political subdivision
18. Service performed by a student for a school, college, or university if he is enrolled and regularly attending classes.
19. Certain services performed by a student under the age of 22 who is enrolled at a nonprofit or public educational institution which combines academic instruction with work experience
20. Service performed by a patient of a hospital for the hospital

Administration

The Texas Employment Commission is appointed by the governor to administer the Act. The three members, representing labor, management, and the public, are appointed for six years. The Texas State Employment Service is a division of the commission, maintaining free public employment offices in more than ninety cities, (R.C.S. Art. 5221f8).

Texas has reciprocal arrangements with other states. The unemployed worker is thereby enabled to apply for benefits earned in one state after he has moved to another state. The amount and duration of benefits are determined by the state where he was previously employed.

Claims

The last employer is mailed a notice of the filing of an initial claim. If the initial claim is filed in Texas, a copy (Form B-3, Initial

Claim for Benefits) will be mailed from the local office which accepted it. If the initial claim is accepted in another state, a form letter (FL-11) will be mailed from the state office in Austin.

An employer should protest a claim when knowledge of any facts is available that may adversely affect the claimant's right to receive unemployment insurance or that may affect a charge to the employer's account. The law provides that an employer has 12 days from the date the notice is mailed in which to mail or deliver a protest to the office from which notice of the claim was mailed.

When a protest is received from an employer, the employer will be mailed a copy of the determination made in regard to the claim (Form B-33, Notice of Claim Determination). If the claimant received the wages from a taxed employer who is an interested party, and if such wages were used to establish his claim, Form B-33 will also indicate whether the benefits paid to the claimant during his benefit year will be charged to the account of such interested party.

If the claimant does not have sufficient wages to qualify for unemployment insurance, the interested party will be mailed a letter providing this information.

Either the employer, if he is an interested party, or the claimant can file an appeal. Each has 12 days from the date a determination is mailed in which to file an appeal.

The sum of the regular unemployment benefits paid and 50% of the extended benefits paid to a claimant and charged to the tax account(s) of his base-period employer(s) is called a "chargeback." Chargebacks are used to compute an employer's tax rate and are not an amount owed by the employer.

If a claimant does not draw all of the benefits for which he qualifies, the benefits not drawn will not become chargebacks. If at any time following the initial claim date an employer knows of circumstances which would prevent payment to the claimant, the employer should notify the commission in writing of the circumstances and mail such notification to the Texas Employment Commission, Insurance Department, TEC Building, Austin, Texas 78778.

After a claimant is paid his first insurance payment, Form C-66, Notice of Maximum Potential Chargeback, is mailed to each of his base-period taxed employers. The form shows the maximum amount of unemployment benefits potentially chargeable to the employer's account for tax-computation purposes.

The taxed employer to whom Form C-66 is mailed has 12 days from the date the form is mailed in which to protest the chargeback notice and present facts which will prevent his account from being charged with benefits paid to the claimant. If such an employer is the employer for whom the claimant last worked prior to his initial claim date, he will have been notified previously of the claim and will have no further right to protest the chargeback notice except for any clerical or machine error as to the amount of the maximum potential chargeback.

The lower part of Form C-66, Notice of Maximum Potential Chargeback, should be used by the employer to protest the chargeback. This part of Form C-66 is Form B-115, Employer Protest to Chargeback Notice. The employer should complete it in detail and mail it to the Texas Employment Commission, Chargeback Determination Unit, TEC Building, Austin, Texas 78778, within 12 days after the date Form C-66 is mailed.

An employer can file a protest to a Notice of Maximum Potential Chargeback when the claimant's last separation from work with the employer prior to the initial claim date shown on Form C-66 was under one of the following circumstances:

1. The claimant's separation was required by a federal or Texas statute or a Texas municipal ordinance.
2. The claimant left his work voluntarily without good cause connected with his work.
3. The claimant was discharged for misconduct connected with his work.

When a determination is made with respect to a protest, the employer is mailed Form B-78, Notice of Decision of Potential Chargeback. Form B-78 will show whether the claimant's benefits are chargeable or not chargeable to the employer's account. If the employer desires to appeal the decision, he has 12 days after the date Form B-78 is mailed in which to do so.

When an appeal is received from either the employer or the claimant, the Appeal Tribunal schedules a hearing and notifies all interested parties of the time and place of the hearing.

The appeals referee considers the record and testimony and renders a written decision. The decision includes the statement of the facts in issue, the applicable law, and the basis for the referee's decision. Copies of the decision are mailed to all interested parties. Further appeal may be made to the commission within the ten days after the mailing of the Appeal Tribunal decision.

When an appeal is received by the commission, and it has rendered a decision, a request for reconsideration may be made to the commission within ten days after the date of the decision. If a request for reconsideration is not made to the commission, appeal may be made to any court of competent jurisdiction in the county of the claimant's residence after the tenth day following the date of the commission's decision and must be made before the end of the twentieth day.

4

Workers' Compensation

Enactment and General Provisions

The purpose of the Texas Workers' Compensation Act is to provide prompt payment of benefits to an employee or his survivor for work-related disease, injury, or death, regardless of fault or cause.

Workers' compensation insurance is compulsory in 27 states and elective in the other 23 states. Texas has an elective law whereby the employer may deline coverage under the act, but may be sued without recourse to the usual common-law defenses of assumed risks of the job, the negligence of fellow servants, and the contributory negligence of the employee. If the employer is a subscriber to the state workers' compensation insurance, the employee or his beneficiary has a right to compensation under the law. Employees whose employer is not a subscriber are entitled to bring suit and may recover judgment against the employer for all damages resulting from injury on the job (R.C.S. Art. 8306).

The Workers' Compensation Law was first enacted in 1917, amended to 1977. It is administered by a three-member Industrial Accident Board appointed by the governor. Employees file compensation claims with the board, which hears cases and makes awards. Cases may be appealed thereafter to the Court of Civil Appeals. The board handles 85,000 to 125,000 claims a year. The majority of decisions are settled out of court under a new pilot system which institutes a regional pretrial conference.

The Texas Employer's Insurance Association was created under the law, which also provides that any insurance company may write workers' compensation insurance (R.C.S. Art. 8308).

Exclusions

The following injuries are not included as "injury sustained in the course of employment" (R.C.S. Art. 8309-1):

1. Injury caused by act of God
2. Injury caused by third person because of personal reasons and not as an employee
3. Injury received while intoxicated
4. Injury caused by employee's willful intention to injure himself or someone else

Compensation for hernia is allowed when there was an injury resulting in hernia, and the hernia appeared immediately following the injury. When the hernia is repaired by surgery the employee is entitled to 26 weeks of compensation in addition to medical bills, even if he returns to work sooner. If the surgery is unsuccessful, the employee is entitled to compensation for the duration of incapacity, but not to exceed 401 weeks (R.C.S. Art. 8306).

Covered Employment

All employers of one or more employees are covered by the Act, except agricultural, labor, and domestic service.

The state is self-insuring. All political subdivisions of the state must become either self-insurers, provide insurance under workers' compensation insurance, or combine with other political subdivisions for self-insurance.

Railway employees are covered by a separate law.

Voluntary coverage of sole proprietors and partnerships is permitted.

When an employer is a subscriber to the insurance association or carrier, the employees are limited to the compensation provided by the Workers' Compensation Act. The employee or his survivors may sue the employer only in the following circumstances: (1) the employer is not a subscriber, (2) the employer is a subscriber, and the employee has declared within the first five days of employment that he will decline coverage under Workers' Compensation in order to reserve his rights under common law, and (3) the surviving heirs are compensated under workers' compensation, but they may sue for exemplary damages if the employee's death was caused by the willful act or omission or gross negligence of the employer (R.C.S. Art. 8306).

Benefits

The benefits paid to the injured employee under the Workers' Compensation Act are intended to pay for part of the losses suffered by the work-related accident or illness. These include direct payment of all related medical expenses, compensation for lost wages, and disability benefits. No compensation will be paid for an injury which does not incapacitate the employee for at least a week. In any case, the company is expected to pay for full medical benefits, all the medical aid, hospital, nurses, chiropractors, and medicines as required at the time of the injury and as long thereafter as necessary to treat the injury. Liability for medical treatment of silicosis and asbestosis is limited to 91 days (R.C.S. Arts. 8306-6 and -7).

The employee must notify the employer within 30 days after injury or manifestation of occupational disease, and file a claim with the Industrial Accident Board within 6 months of the date of injury, or date of employer's report to the board. If the company fails to furnish medical aid when needed after notice of the injury, the injured employee may obtain the medical care at the expense of the employer. The employee has the right to call in any doctor to administer first aid and furnish subsequent treatment at the expense of the company. All medical fees are subject to regulation of the board. The treating doctor is required to file a medical report with the Industrial Accident Board, the insurance company, and the injured worker. Medical treatment includes rehabilitation, and fitting and training in the use of prosthetic appliances (R.C.S. Art. 8306-7). This includes replacement or repair of the artificial appliances.

While an employee is totally disabled for more than seven days, the company must pay compensation benefits equal to 66⅔% of his average weekly wage, with a maximum of $91 and a minimum of $19 effective October 1, 1977. Thereafter, maximum benefits will increase $7, and minimum benefits will increase $1, for every $10 increase in state-wide average weekly earnings of the previous year, as published by the Texas Employment Commission. Weekly benefits for total incapacity can continue up to 401 weeks after the date of injury. Compensation for partial disability is 66⅔% of the difference between his former and present earnings, to a maximum of $63 per week, for a period no greater than 300 weeks (R.C.S. Art. 8306-10 and 11).

Specific compensation is allowed for particular losses in lieu of all other payments. The following are total and permanent incapacity cases compensable for 401 weeks (R.C.S. Art. 8306-11a):

1. Loss of sight of both eyes
2. Loss of both feet
3. Loss of both hands
4. Loss of one hand and one foot
5. Paralysis of both arms, both legs, or one arm and one leg
6. Incurable insanity or imbecility resulting from an injury

Benefits for other specific injuries are established at 60% of the weekly wage for the number of weeks indicated below (R.C.S. Art. 8306-12):

300 weeks—loss of an eye and a foot
150 weeks—loss of hearing (complete)
60 weeks—loss of a thumb
45 weeks—loss of an index finger
30 weeks—loss of a second finger or a great toe
21 weeks—loss of a third finger
15 weeks—loss of a fourth finger
150 weeks—loss of the hand
200 weeks—loss of an arm or a leg
125 weeks—loss of a foot
100 weeks—loss of sight of one eye

Vocational Rehabilitation

Employers must notify the Texas Workers' Compensation Board of each injury covered under the law. The board in turn will inform the injured employee of the services available to him under the Vocational Rehabilitation Commission. This recommendation by the board is made after consultation with the employee's doctor.

Beneficiaries

The beneficiaries of the death benefit may be among the following: surviving husband (or wife) who has not abandoned his wife (or husband) at the time of the injury and for a period of three years prior thereto; minor children, parents and stepmother, without regard to dependency; dependent grandparents, children, grandchildren, brothers and sisters of the deceased employee. The amount of compensation is distributed among the beneficiaries according to the laws of descent and distribution in Texas. The compensation is not liable for the debts of the deceased or the beneficiaries, and is paid directly to the beneficiaries rather than to the estate of the deceased (R.C.S. Art. 8306-8a).

Death benefits to the legal beneficiaries amount to 66⅔% of the employee's average weekly earnings to the maximum weekly benefit. The spouse's portion is one-half, and the minor children's portion is one-half of the benefit amount. The spouse's portion continues until remarriage, in which case he or she receives a lump sum payment equal to two years of benefit. The minor's portion continues until the age of 18 (or 25 for full-time students in an accredited educational institution). When any of the beneficiaries becomes ineligible to receive benefits, the balance reverts to the other beneficiaries. If neither spouse nor child survives the deceased worker, then other beneficiaries are entitled to weekly benefits for a period of 360 weeks.

In case death occurs as a result of the injury after a period for which disability compensation was paid, the amounts paid are deducted from the death benefit.

Funeral expenses not to exceed $1,250 are remitted to the person who paid for the funeral.

If there are no beneficiaries, payment is made into the second injury fund.

Financing

Employers are required to pay all premiums for workers' compensation insurance, at rates approved by the State Board of Insurance. It is illegal to collect from employees any part of the premium paid on any policy under this law (R.C.S. Art. 8306-12g).

Second Injury Fund

If an employee who has suffered a previous injury incurs a subsequent injury, which results in any incapacity to which both injuries have contributed, the insurance company is liable for the entire case. However, the company can claim reimbursement from the second injury fund for the excess of total incapacity over the second injury. The fund is financed by requiring the association to pay the Industrial Accident Board the full death benefit where there is no survivor entitled to compensation. The insurance company is liable for a set limit on specified injuries and second injuries. The fund pays the balance of 401 weeks (R.C.S. Art. 8306-12c).

Attorney's Fees

Attorney's fees are subject to approval of the Industrial Accident Board, and are limited to 25% of the total compensation plus reasonable expenses. Attorneys' fees regulated by the trial court are likewise set at a maximum of 25% of the amount recovered. In fatal cases where there is no issue as to liability or beneficiary, the court allows only expenses (R.C.S. Art. 8306-7c and d).

Filing a Claim

An injured worker or his employer must notify the insurance company, which will process the claim. If the claim is disputed, Industrial Accident Board prehearing examiners hold conferences in regional offices with representatives of the insurance company and the employee, in order to hear the case before presentation to the board in Austin. If the parties disagree, the case goes to the Industrial Accident Board in Austin. Their decision can be appealed to the state district court.

Regional offices of the Texas Industrial Accident Board are located in Beaumont, Corpus Christi, Dallas, El Paso, Fort Worth, Houston, Lubbock, Odessa, San Antonio, and Tyler.

Confidentiality of Records

The information in a worker's claim is confidential and may not be disclosed except under circumstances delineated below.

If there is a claim pending, the claimant's name, age, social security number, date of injury and names of private employers must be given on request *only* to the claimant, the claimant's attorney, the insurance carrier, the employer at time of injury, third party litigants, or the State Board of Insurance.

All information of the Industrial Accident Board on a person who has been finally adjudicated to be a fraudulent claimant is *not* confidential, and shall be furnished to anyone on request.

If an applicant for employment has had three or more general injury claims filed in the preceding five years, the applicant may provide written authorization to release information to a prospective employer regarding the date and nature of injury to the applicant.

Whenever a claimant makes a fifth claim for compensation within any five-year period, the Industrial Accident Board notifies the attorney general, who will investigate for possible fraud.

5

Occupational Safety and Health

Occupational Safety

The Williams-Steiger Occupational Safety and Health Act of 1970 (OSHA), which became effective on April 28, 1971, is the first federal legislation in this area. The law permits the secretary of labor to approve state plans for administration and enforcement of state standards provided they are equally as effective as federal standards. However, the Texas Occupational Safety Act of 1967 does not meet the required enforcement procedures of the federal law.

Federal Legislation

The provisions of the OSHA apply to all employers engaged in a business affecting commerce. Federal, state, and local government employees are excluded from coverage. However, each federal agency must establish and maintain an occupational safety and health program consistent with OSHA standards. State plans must include an occupational safety and health program applicable to all employees of public agencies of the state and its political subdivisions, which program is as effective as the standards contained in an approved plan. The terms of the OSHA do not apply to working conditions protected under other federal occupational safety and health laws such as those under the Federal Coal Mine Health and

Safety Act, and under the Atomic Energy Act. Self-employed persons and family-owned and operated farms are not covered under the Act.

Duties. The main requirements of the law are that: (1) each employer shall furnish a place of employment which is free from recognized hazards that are likely to cause death or serious physical harm to his employee, and he shall comply with occupational safety and health standards promulgated under the act; and (2) each employee shall comply with occupational safety and health standards, and all regulations issued pursuant to the act which are applicable to his own actions and conduct.

Standards. The secretary of labor is authorized to promulgate as occupational safety and health standards, any existing federal standard, or any national consensus standards; revise, modify, or revoke existing standards; and promulgate new ones. The secretary is required to publish in the Federal Register a statement of his reasons for any action he takes to promulgate standards, issue orders, grant exemptions, or settle any penalty assessed under the act. Single copies of standards are available free from any OSHA office.

Complaints of violations. Any employees or their representatives who believe that a violation of a job safety or health standard exists which threatens physical harm, may request an inspection by sending a signed written notice to the Department of Labor. The names of the complainants need not be furnished to the employer. The secretary is required to notify the complainants in writing, and to set up procedures for informal review, in a case where a citation is not issued.

Enforcement. In enforcing the standards, Labor Department safety inspectors may enter at reasonable times any establishment covered by the Act. When an inspection reveals a violation, the employer is issued a written citation or notice describing the violation and setting a reasonable time for correction of the violation. The citation must be posted at or near the place where the violation occurred.

Penalties. The employer is notified by mail of the penalty, if any, which will be assessed. Willful or repeated violations may incur penalties of up to $10,000. An employer who fails to correct a violation for which a citation has been issued may be fined up to $1,000 each day. Willful violation by an employer which results in death of an employee is punishable by a fine of up to $10,000 or imprisonment for up to six months.

Variances. Employers may apply to OSHA for a temporary variance from a standard if they are unable to comply by a required date, or for a permanent variance if they prefer their own standards.

Recordkeeping requirements. Employers are required to keep records and make periodic reports on work-related deaths, injuries, illnesses, and employee exposure to toxic materials. If an on-the-job accident kills one employee or hospitalizes five or more employees, this must be reported to the nearest OSHA office within 48 hours. Otherwise, employers with fewer than ten employees are exempt from recordkeeping requirements of the Act.

State Legislation

The Texas Occupational Safety Act of 1967 applied to all employees except carriers regulated by the Interstate Commerce Commission. The federal law (OSHA) preempted the state from enforcement of the state law. However, the Texas Division of Occupational Safety may act as a consultant to private employers. OSHA will pay 90% of the cost of sending state consultants to a workplace to identify unsafe conditions upon the request of an employer.

Migrant Labor Camps

The Texas Department of Health is required to license and regulate migrant labor camps in the state, beginning July 1971. These are defined as living quarters for 15 or more seasonal, temporary, or migrant agricultural workers. Licenses are obtained after inspection by the state commissioner of health, for an annual fee of $15 to $50 based on the number of beds or housing units.

If the camp does not meet inspection standards, the commissioner can issue a temporary permit for a maximum of six months to allow time to prepare the camp to pass inspection.

The license may be suspended or revoked for violation of the law or the rules and regulations promulgated by the State Board of Health prescribing standards for living quarters at the camps. This may include provisions relating to sanitary conditions, water, toilets, garbage, light, air, and safety to protect health and safety of occupants.

Persons operating a migrant camp without a license are subject to a maximum of 30 days in jail and/or a fine of $100. Employees or occupants who do not use the sanitary facilities furnished, or who vandalize or misuse the facilities are subject to a fine of not more than $25. For a second violation the maximum penalty is 30 days and/or $100.

The commissioner of health may apply to the district court for a temporary or permanent injunction to prevent violation of the act (Ref. H.B. No. 1254, May 1971).

6

Payroll Deductions

Employers are required to deduct income tax and social security taxes from workers' gross pay, and to forward payments to the appropriate government agency. Private deductions such as union dues and charitable contributions may be deducted by mutual agreement of employer and employee. The employer is required to furnish an itemized statement of gross pay, itemized deductions, and net pay with each paycheck.

Employment Taxes

Every employer who pays wages to employees for services performed is responsible for withholding, paying, and reporting of federal income tax, social security (FICA) taxes, and unemployment tax (see Chapter 3 on unemployment insurance).

Every employer must have an employer identification number, available by application to any office of the Internal Revenue Service or Social Security Administration. Every employee must have a social security number, available by application on Form SS-4 to any office of the Social Security Administration or Internal Revenue Service.

Taxable Wages

Taxable wages include all remuneration for services performed. This includes salaries, vacation allowances, supplemental unemployment benefits, bonuses, and commissions. The following payments are treated as exceptions:

1. Wages paid in any form other than cash are measured by the fair market value of the goods, meals, etc. given in payment.
2. Amounts paid for traveling and other reimbursed expenses on the job are not taxable wages, and must be identified separately. Moving expenses are not subject to withholding tax if it is reasonable to believe that the employee is entitled to an income tax deduction.
3. Cash tips must be reported to the employer monthly. The employee must submit either Form 4070 reporting tips, or a statement showing his name, address, social security number, employer's name and address, month of statement, and total amount of tips. The employer must collect both social security tax and income tax on tips reported. The employer must pay social security tax on employee tips only up to the federal minimum wage.
4. Social security taxes apply to all *cash* wages paid to a household employee in any calendar quarter in which the employee receives at least $50 during the quarter. This does not apply to members of the immediate family. The value of food, lodging, clothing is not subject to social security tax. If an employer files Form 941 for business employees, household employees may be included. Otherwise, they are reported on Form 942.
5. Wages of newspaper carriers under 18 years of age delivering to consumers are exempt from all employment tax.

Tax Rates

Income tax withholding. Each new employee should complete Form W-4, Employee's Withholding Allowance Certificate, when he starts to work, and file a new form whenever his number of exemptions changes. This indicates the number of withholding allowances claimed, as a basis for determination of the amount of income tax to withhold according to wage-bracket tables furnished by the Internal Revenue Service.

Federal unemployment tax. The federal unemployment tax is 3.4% of wages paid up to $6,000 for each employee. Contributions into state unemployment insurance funds are credited against the federal tax for up to 2.7% of taxable wages. This tax cannot be deducted from the wages of employees.

Quarterly Returns—Form 941

Every employer who withholds income tax or social security taxes must file a quarterly return with the Internal Revenue Service Center for the region of his legal residence or place of business. (The IRS Center in Austin, Texas, covers the states of Arkansas, Kansas, Louisiana, New Mexico, Oklahoma, and Texas.) The returns are due within 30 days of the end of the calendar quarter on the appropriate form. Form 941 is required to be filed by all employers, with these exemptions:

1. Form 941E is used for state and local government employees and tax-exempt organizations that report only withheld income tax, and not social security tax. Information on reporting social security tax may be obtained from the Texas Department of Public Welfare.
2. Form 942 may be used for reporting taxes on wages of household employees (941 may also be used).
3. Form 943 must be used for reporting taxes on wages of agricultural employees.

Employers may submit reports on magnetic tape instead of the above forms, in accordance with instructions available from the Social Security Administration and the Internal Revenue Service.

Tax Payments

Income taxes withheld and social security taxes must be deposited with an authorized commercial bank depository or a Federal Reserve Bank. Federal Tax Deposit Form 501 must accompany each deposit (Form 511 for agricultural labor). Deposits are made according to the amount of income tax and social security taxes due:

1. If the amount due is less than $200, you may either pay the taxes directly to Internal Revenue, using Form 941, or make a bank deposit with Form 501.
2. If the amount due at the end of the quarter is $200 or more, you

must deposit the entire amount with the Federal Reserve or authorized depository bank within 30 days.

3. If at the end of any month the amount of undeposited taxes is $200 or more but less than $2,000, the taxes must be deposited within 3 banking days after the end of the quarter-month.

State and local government employers should deposit withheld income tax only. Any social security contribution should be sent to the Texas Department of Public Welfare.

Both criminal and civil penalties are provided for willful failure to file returns or willful filing of false returns.

Annual Returns—Form 940

Every employer must file an annual unemployment tax return on Form 940, and deposit or pay the tax in full. Forms are mailed to employers who filed returns for the previous year, and are also available from the IRS. The federal unemployment tax must be deposited with a Federal Reserve bank or commercial bank depository. A Federal Tax Deposit Form 508 must accompany each deposit of federal unemployment tax.

Employers must furnish employees with a statement of wages paid and taxes collected on Form W-2, if compensation plus wages amount to $600 or more in a calendar year. If wages were also subject to social security tax (FICA), Form W-2 must show the FICA wages paid and tax withheld. If wages are less than $600, the employer may give the information on Form W-2, Form SS-14, or a statement containing the employer's name and identification; employee's name, address, and social security number; total FICA wages paid and FICA employee tax withheld during the year. If the employment is terminated during the year, the statement must be given to the employee within 30 days after his last wages are paid. Privately printed forms may be substituted for Form W-2 to provide additional information on other voluntary payroll deductions. Reports may be submitted on magnetic tape (see Revenue Procedures 71-18 and 71-20).

All records pertaining to employment taxes should be kept available for inspection by the Internal Revenue Service, for a period of at least four years after the date the taxes are due.

7

Social Security and Retirement

Federal retirement, survivors', and disability benefits, and hospital insurance benefits are paid for by contributions based on earnings covered under social security. This is a national insurance system whereby the employed pay social security contributions which are pooled in special trust funds. When earnings stop because the worker retires, dies, or becomes disabled, monthly cash benefits are paid to the family.

Wages or self-employment income of $400 or more a year are entered on individual records by the Social Security Administration. This earnings record is used to determine eligibility and amount of cash benefits. Questions about contributions or refunds for excess contributions (when you have had more than one employer in a year) should be directed to the Internal Revenue Service.

Social Security

Contributions

The contribution rate in 1978 is 12.1% of all earnings up to $17,700 per year. The employer deducts 6.05% from the gross pay of each employee and contributes a matching 6.05%. For self-employed people, the total contribution rate is 8.1%. The wage base and contribution rate will increase gradually up to 7.15% each for employers and employees, and 10% for self-employed. See Table 7.1.

Table 7.1
Social Security Taxes

Year	Employer and Employee (each)	Self-Employed	Wage Base
1977	5.85%	7.90%	$16,500
1978	6.05	8.10	17,700
1979	6.13	8.10	22,900
1980	6.13	8.10	25,900
1981	6.65	9.30	29,700
1982	6.70	9.35	31,800
1983	6.70	9.35	33,900
1984	6.70	9.35	36,000
1985	7.05	9.90	38,100
1986	7.15	10.00	40,200

In Texas the state will pay on behalf of its employees the employee share of contributions not to exceed 5.85% of wages, up to $16,500 in any calendar year, beginning September 1, 1978.

Who Is Covered?

Almost all paid employment and self-employment is covered by social security with the following exceptions:

1. Farm operators are covered by social security if they net at least $400 per year. For social security purposes, if your annual gross earnings from farming are between $600 and $2,400, you may report two-thirds of your *gross* earnings for social security purposes. If your gross earnings are more than $2,400 and your net earnings are less than $1,600 you may report $1,600 for social security purposes. This optional method enables the farmer to maintain social security coverage in years of low income or losses. You receive social security credits for farm rental income only if you "materially participate" in farm production. Farm employees earn social security credits when they earn $150 or more in cash from each employer, or if they do farm work for the employer on twenty or more days during the year for cash wages figured on a time basis (not piece-rates).
2. Self-employment income from nonfarm business is covered if

net income is at least $400 in at least two of the three prior taxable years. The contributor may use two-thirds of gross income, up to $1,600, for social security purposes. The option allows self-employed persons to receive higher social security credit than their net earnings would allow in prior years, and therefore provides a higher future benefit amount.

3. Income of clergymen was not covered by social security before 1968 unless the individual filed a form requesting coverage. Beginning in 1968, earnings are automatically covered unless the clergyman applies for exclusion on the basis of conscientious opposition by reason of religious principles. Members of a religious order who have taken a vow of poverty are exempt from social security.
4. A domestic worker in a private household is covered if cash wages amount to $50 or more from one employer in a calendar quarter.
5. Employees of nonprofit religious, charitable, and educational organizations may be covered by the social security law if the organization waives its exemption (by filing Form SS-15 with the Internal Revenue Service); and those employees earning $50 or more in a quarter desiring coverage sign Form SS-15a, which accompanies this certificate.
6. Employees of the federal government are covered by social security if not covered by the Civil Service Retirement System. All state employees in Texas, including employees of institutions of higher education, are covered. Local government employees may be covered by voluntary agreement.
7. Military service counts toward social security, although no social security taxes were collected before 1957. Social security credits of $160 a month are given for military service between September 15, 1940 and December 31, 1956. For active duty after 1957, credits amount to basic pay plus $100 per month (up to the maximum taxable earning for civilians).
8. Railroad employment is covered by the Railroad Retirement Act, not the Social Security Act. A retired worker who has at least ten years of railroad service and five years social security credit (six years by 1975), may receive benefits under both railroad retirement and social security. Survivors can receive benefits under only one system, but earnings of the deceased

worker under both systems are combined to determine survivor benefits.

9. U.S. citizens employed by American employers in foreign countries, or on vessels or aircraft of foreign registry, are covered by the Social Security Act. U.S. citizens working abroad for a foreign subsidiary of an American corporation are covered if the parent firm makes an agreement with the secretary of the treasury that all U.S. citizen employees will be covered.
10. Foreign workers in the United States are generally covered. Seamen and airmen employed on American vessels or aircrafts are covered. Temporary foreign agriculture workers are not covered. Foreign visitors are not covered for work performed under a foreign exchange program, but may be covered for other employment.
11. Tips of $20 or more per month with one employer are covered. The amount of tips is reported to the employer each month. The social security tax on these tips can be deducted from the employee's wages, or paid to the employer by the employee. The employer forwards the contribution to the IRS, and adds a matching contribution.

Types of Cash Benefits

Social security benefits are payable to retired workers, disabled workers, and survivors.

Retirement. Monthly payments to a retired worker at age 65 (reduced benefits as early as 62); unmarried children under 18 (or under 22 if fulltime students); unmarried disabled children 18 or over who were severely disabled before 22; wife or husband 62 or over; wife under 62 caring for qualified worker's child.

Survivors. Monthly payments to a deceased worker's unmarried children under 18 (or 22 if full-time students, or severely disabled before age 22); widow or widower 60 or older; widow, widower, or surviving divorced mother if caring for worker's children; widow or widower age 50 or older who becomes disabled within 7 years after worker's death or within 7 years after termination of checks received for caring for worker's child; dependent parents 62 or older.

Disability. Monthly payments to the disabled worker and his dependents.

Divorce. If the marriage lasted 10 years or more, a divorced wife may receive benefits at age 62, a surviving divorced wife at 60, or a disabled surviving divorced wife at 50 or older.

Monthly Retirement or Disability Benefits

A worker is eligible for full retirement benefits at the age of 65, or 80% of benefits at the age of 62. Workers are *fully* insured if they have credit for one-quarter year of work for each year after 1950 up to the year benefits are claimed. The minimum credit is for one and one-half years of work, and the maximum required is ten years of work. Workers are *currently* insured if they have credit for at least one and one-half years within the three years prior to the benefit claim. Most types of cash benefits require only that the worker be *fully insured.* However, currently insured *or* fully insured status qualifies a child, widow, widower, or surviving divorced mother with an entitled child in their care for survivor benefits and lump-sum death payment. To get disability benefits the worker needs credit for 5 years of work in the 10 years before becoming disabled; or if a worker becomes disabled before the age of 31, he needs social security credits for half the time after the age of 21.

Monthly cash payments are based on average earnings creditable for social security. A worker who will reach 65 in 1978 who has always paid the maximum social security taxes, would compute average earning as follows:

1. List taxable earnings since 1959 (omitting five lowest years 1954-1958):

1959-65	$ 33,600	(4,800 × 7)
1966-67	13,200	(6,600 × 2)
1968-71	31,200	(7,800 × 4)
1972	9,000	
1973	10,800	
1974	13,200	
1975	14,100	
1976	15,300	
1977	16,500	
	$156,900	

2. Divide earnings by 19 years. The result is \$8,257 average taxable earnings. This will provide benefits of approximately \$460 per month for a worker retired at 65, \$368 at 62. A wife 65 or older and dependent children would receive an additional 50% each up to a maximum family payment of \$804. Survivors benefits would be \$329 for a widow or dependent widower at 60, \$381 for a widow or widower at 62, \$690 for a widowed mother or father and one dependent child, and \$345 for one surviving child.

Social security benefits increase automatically with increases in the cost of living.

Employment after Retirement

The earnings of employees who are receiving social security benefits are subject to the same employment taxes as those of other employees. However, the cash benefits may be reduced. One dollar in benefits is withheld for each two dollars in earnings above \$4,000 (\$3,240 for beneficiaries under 65). The earnings limit will be increased to \$4,500 in 1979, to \$5,000 in 1980, to \$5,500 in 1981, and \$6,000 in 1982. No benefits are forfeited for wages earned after the age of 72 (age 70 in 1982).

If retirement is delayed after age 65, benefits are increased 1% for each year up to the age of 72 (3% starting in 1982).

Medicare

Medicare. If you are 65 or over and eligible for social security or railroad retirement benefits, you are automatically eligible for hospital insurance. If you reached 65 before 1968 you are eligible for hospital insurance even if you are ineligible for cash social security benefits. If you reached 65 after 1968, you will need some work credit to qualify for hospital insurance benefits. Medical insurance is voluntary, and financed jointly by the individual and the government. The monthly premium is \$8.20 as of July 1, 1978.

Hospital Insurance

Part A of Medicare, hospital insurance, is financed by social security taxes and is available to nearly everyone 65 and over upon application. This includes anyone 65 or over entitled to social security or railroad retirement benefits, whether he draws these benefits; disabled persons under 65 who have been receiving social security or railroad retirement benefits for 24 months; persons with chronic renal disease; and persons who reached 65 before 1968 who are not eligible for cash social security benefits. Persons ineligible for social security at age 65 can obtain hospital insurance for a monthly premium of $54.

Hospital insurance pays the cost of covered services for:

1. Hospitalization up to 60 days in each benefit period except for the first $144; for the sixty-first to ninetieth day, except for $36 a day; a lifetime reserve of 60 additional days, except for $72 a day. A new benefit period begins when you have not been in a hospital or nursing facility for 60 days consecutively.
2. Care for 100 days in each benefit period in an extended-care facility, if you are admitted within 14 days after discharge from a hospital where you were a patient for at least 3 consecutive days. All covered services are paid for the first 20 days, and all but $18 a day for the next 80 days.
3. A total of 100 home health visits by nurses, physical therapists or other health workers, if a plan for care is established by a doctor within 14 days of your discharge from the hospital or extended-care facility.

Medical Insurance

Part B of Medicare, medical insurance, is a voluntary program financed by monthly premiums of $7.70 ($8.20 as of July 1978) which are supplemented by the government. People who became eligible for hospital insurance after July 1973, are automatically covered unless they decline. Prior to that date, it was necessary to enroll within a specified time period. Persons ineligible for cash social security benefits who enroll for Part A must also enroll for Part B.

Medical insurance pays for 80% of the reasonable charges (after the first $60 a year) of doctors, physical therapists, laboratory service, colostomy care supplies, certain services of chiropractors and podiatrists, and other health services; home health care after an annual $60 deductible, up to 100 visits per year; and hemodialysis treatment (after three months of treatment) or a kidney transplant for persons insured under social security, and their dependents.

For further information, read *Your Medicare Handbook* available free from any social security administration office.

Private Employee Benefit Plans

Private employee pension and welfare benefit plans are regulated by the Employee Retirement Income Security Act of 1974 (ERISA). ERISA applies to any employee benefit plan provided by an employer engaged in or affecting commerce or by an employee organization representing employees engaged in or affecting commerce. The law requires disclosure of the provisions of the welfare or pension plan and establishes standards of conduct for trustees and administrators. For pension plans, it establishes funding, participation, and vesting requirements, and makes termination insurance available through the Pension Benefit Guaranty Corporation. It also permits employees not covered by a pension plan to set aside tax-free income in an individual retirement account. However, the Act does not require employers to offer pension plans.

An employee *welfare* plan may provide any of the following benefits: medical, accident, disability, death, unemployment, vacation, scholarship, apprenticeship or other training, prepaid legal services, holiday pay, severance pay, and other benefits.

An employee *pension benefit* plan may provide retirement benefits for age and service, disability retirement benefits, retirement benefits through profit sharing, stock bonuses, thrift plans, income beyond termination of employment, and joint and survivor annuity.

Contributions to a plan may be made individually or jointly by employers, employee organizations, or employees. Keogh plans established under Section 401(a) of the Internal Revenue Code, which do not cover any employees (other than self-employed individuals or partners), and individual retirement accounts, described in Sections 408(a) and (b) and 409 of the Internal Revenue Code, are not considered employee pension benefit plans under ERISA.

Reports

Reports must be filed by the plan administrator or sponsor, and plan information must be furnished to participants and beneficiaries.

Plan administrators must file (1) a Plan Description (Form EBS-1) and an annual financial report with the U.S. Department of Labor, (2) an annual report and notice of intent to withdraw from or terminate a plan with the Pension Benefit Guaranty Corporation for plans covered by termination insurance, and (3) an annual financial report with the Internal Revenue Service.

The plan administrators must furnish automatically to participants and beneficiaries a summary plan description and changes thereto, and summary of the annual report. The complete description and report must be made available at the principal office of the administrator. Each participant must be provided upon termination of employment with statement of amount of deferred vested benefits and total benefits accrued. Each participant must be furnished with terms of any annuity and a written explanation of claim denial.

Upon written request, the plan administrator must also furnish free within 30 days an annual statement of benefits accrued and vested; and must furnish at reasonable charge within 30 days, latest updated plan description, annual report, and documents under which the plan is operated.

The plan description and the summary plan must include eligibility requirements, provisions for vesting, conditions for denial of benefits, procedure for presenting claims for benefits, and remedies for appeal.

The annual report must include financial statements showing current value of plan assets and liabilities; receipts and expenditures; employer contributions, detailed information on transactions that exceed 3% of total assets or transactions with parties of interest (i.e., plan administrator, employer, plan employees); insurance and actuarial information; and the opinion of an independent accountant.

Participation, Vesting, and Funding

A pension plan must allow an employee to participate when he or she is age 25 and has completed one year of service. A plan requiring full and immediate vesting may require an employee to put in three years of service. An employee may be excluded if he or she begins employment within five years of the normal retirement age.

"Vesting" is the right to pension benefits the employee has earned even though he or she has left that job before retirement. A pension plan must provide full vesting of employee contributions. Employer contributions must vest at least 50% after 10 years, and 100% after 15 years of service. Exemption from the vesting rules is allowed for certain plans with no employer contributions, or plans which provide deferred compensation for top management.

ERISA requires employers to fund pension credits as employees earn them, and to fund for past service liabilities according to a formula.

Exemptions

Welfare plans covering fewer than 100 participants, which satisfy certain criteria, need not file reports with the U.S. Department of Labor unless specifically requested for certain documents, nor furnish participants with a summary of the annual report, nor a copy of the plan description. However, they must furnish participants and beneficiaries with an updated summary plan description.

Welfare plans covering fewer than 100 participants which are part of a group insurance arrangement must file an annual report with the U.S. Department of Labor. They must furnish participants and beneficiaries with updated summary plan description, summary of annual report, and written explanation of claims denial.

Welfare plans financed and maintained by the employer to provide benefits for a select management group are exempted from all the reporting and disclosure requirements except to provide plan documents to the secretary of labor upon request.

Fiduciary Standards

ERISA requires the fiduciary (person who exercises discretionary control over plan management or assets) to perform in the best interests of the participants and beneficiaries. This requires investment according to the "prudent man rule," diversifying plan investments and limiting investment in employer securities and real property.

Pension Plan Termination Insurance

ERISA requires the insurance of defined benefit pension plans (ones which provide a fixed pension benefit). The plans pay a premium to the Pension Benefit Guaranty Corporation, a corporation established within the U.S. Department of Labor. The uniform premium rate is set so as to provide sufficient revenue to cover its expenditures, but not more than 0.1% of the present value of the plans.

Additional Information

More information is available at the area office of the Labor—Management Services Administration of the U.S. Department of Labor.

Appendix A

Federal and State Laws Affecting Workers

The table that follows summarizes the state and federal laws affecting employers and employees. Included with each law are a brief description of its major provisions, information about who is covered, and who is not covered (specific exemptions), and addresses and telephone numbers of the various offices that may be contacted for further information.

Federal and State Laws Affecting Workers

Federal Law	Major Provisions	Who Is Covered	Specific Exemptions	For Further Information
National Labor Relations Act of 1935, as amended (Wagner and Taft-Hartley Acts)	States the rights of employees to organize and to bargain collectively with their employers through representatives of their own choosing; establishes procedure for NLRB-conducted elections; defines unfair labor practices.	All enterprises whose operation affects interstate commerce; NLRB jurisdiction according to annual gross dollar volume of business—from $50,000 in nonretail operation to $500,000 in retail trade.	Purely local business, government employees, domestic and farm labor, independent contractors, and supervisors.	National Labor Relations Board 819 Taylor Street Fort Worth, Texas 76102 Phone: (817) 334-2921 515 Rusk Street Houston, Texas 77002 Phone: (713) 226-4296 Federal Mediation and Conciliation Service 1200 Main Tower Bldg. Dallas, Texas 75202 Phone: (214) 749-2917 515 Rusk Street Houston, Texas 77002 Phone: (713) 226-4257
Labor-Management Reporting and Disclosure Act of 1959, as amended (Landrum-Griffin Act)	Prescribes rules for election of union officers, rights of union members, trusteeships, handling of union funds and annual financial reports of union.	Labor organizations and their members, employees, labor relations consultants, when engaged in an industry affecting interstate commerce.	State central bodies, local central bodies, and unions consisting exclusively of employees of state governments or their political subdivisions.	Labor Management Services Administration U.S. Department of Labor 555 Griffin Square Dallas, Texas 75202 Phone: (214) 749-2886 Area offices in Corpus Christi, El Paso, Fort Worth, Houston, San

Employee Retirement Income Security Act of 1974	To protect the interests of workers covered by private employee pension and welfare plans and their beneficiaries.	Any employee benefit plan that is established or maintained by an employer or employee organization engaged in interstate commerce.	Government plans; church plans that do not elect coverage; plans maintained solely to comply with workers compensation or unemployment compensation or disability insurance law; excess benefit plans that are unfunded.	Same as above.
Fair Labor Standards Act of 1938, as amended to 1977	Establishes minimum wages and maximum hours, prohibits child labor, and prohibits sex discrimination in wages.	Employees engaged in interstate commerce; in enterprises with gross annual sales volume of $250,000; laundry and cleaners, construction, schools, and hospitals regardless of dollar volume; in federal government; domestic service workers who work 8 hours a week or receive at least $50 in cash wages in a calendar quarter.	Employees of seasonal amusement establishment, farm workers whose employer does not use more than 500 days of labor per quarter; casual baby sitters and companions of the elderly. (Exemption from overtime requirements only to employees of car dealers, radio stations, motion picture theatres, live-in maids.)	Wage and Hour Division Employment Standards Administration U.S. Department of Labor 555 Griffin Square Dallas, Texas 75202 Phone: (214) 749-2037 Area offices in Corpus Christi, El Paso, Fort Worth, Houston, San Antonio, and Waco. Field offices in 19 locations throughout the state.
Davis-Bacon Act of 1935, as amended	Establishes minimum wages on government construction contracts at the prevailing wage for the corresponding class of workers employed locally; and weekly paydays.	Contracts in excess of $2,000, to which the U.S. is a party, for construction and repair of public buildings and public works.	None	Same as above

Federal Law	Major Provisions	Who Is Covered	Specific Exemptions	For Further Information
Walsh-Healey Public Contract Act of 1938, as amended.	Sets basic labor standards for employees working on Government contracts: prevailing wage, overtime pay over 8 hours a day or 40 hours a week; bans child labor and convict labor.	Contracts for manufacture or furnishing of materials or equipment in excess of $10,000.	Common carrier services under published tariff rates, perishables, certain farm products; office and custodial workers.	Same as above
Occupational Safety and Health Act of 1970	Requires employers to furnish a workplace free from recognized safety hazards.	Employers engaged in a business affecting interstate commerce.	Federal, state, and local government employees; self-employed persons; family-owned and operated farms. Employers with fewer than 10 employees are exempt from record keeping requirement only.	Occupational Safety and Health Administration U.S. Department of Labor 555 Griffin Square Dallas, Texas 75202 Phone: (214) 749-2477 Area offices in Austin, Beaumont, Corpus Christi, Dallas, El Paso, Fort Worth, Harlingen, Houston, Lubbock, and San Antonio.
O.A.S.D.H.I. of the Social Security Act of 1935, as amended to 1977.	Provides retirement, survivors, and disability insurance, and health insurance (Medicare) for persons over 65.	Almost all paid employment and self-employment is covered. Farm workers who earn $150 or more in cash; domestic workers who earn $50 or more from one employer in a calendar quarter; self-employed earning $400 or	Federal workers covered under a civil service retirement system, nonprofit organizations which have not waived exemption; news carriers under 18.	Social Security Administration 1200 Main Tower Building Dallas, Texas 75202 Phone: (214) 749-2917 SSA offices in most Texas cities.

Employment Act of 1967.	40 and 65 from age discrimination in hiring, discharge, pay, or other conditions of employment.	persons, employment agencies, and labor organizations.	state, and local governments.	Employment Standards Administration U.S. Department of Labor 555 Griffin Square Dallas, Texas 75202 Phone: (214) 749-2037 Area offices in Corpus Christi, El Paso, Fort Worth, Houston, San Antonio, and Waco.
Title VII of the Civil Rights Act of 1964, as amended by the Equal Employment Opportunity Act of 1972.	Prohibits discrimination based on race, color, religion, sex, and national origin, in all conditions of employment.	Employers of 15 or more employees, employment agencies, labor unions.	Religious organizations, with respect to religious qualifications.	Equal Employment Opportunity Commission 1100 Commerce Street Dallas, Texas 75202 Phone: (214) 749-1841 EEOC district offices located in Dallas, El Paso, Houston, and San Antonio
State Laws				
Texas Minimum Wage Act of 1970	To require wages sufficient for a decent standard of living ($1.40 per hour effective Feb. 1, 1971).	All employers except specific exemptions.	Religious orders, students, executives, domestic servants, seasonal amusement establishments, dairy farmers, employees not covered by the Texas Unemployment Compensation Act (except farm workers).	Texas Department of Labor and Standards Sam Houston Building Capitol Station, Box 12157 Austin, Texas 78711 Phone: (512) 475-2403 Texas Dept. of Agr. P.O. Drawer BB Austin, Texas 78711 Phone: (512) 475-4664

Federal Law	Major Provisions	Who Is Covered	Specific Exemptions	For Further Information
Texas Unemployment Compensation Act of 1935, as amended to 1977	Provides unemployment compensation to workers who are unemployed, financed by a tax on employers.	Any employer who paid wages of $1,500 or more ($20,000 for farm labor) ($4,000 domestic servant); or employed at least 1 person (10 persons for farm labor, 4 persons for non-profit organizations) in each of 20 weeks during the current or preceding calendar year, states and political subdivision are included.	School employees and teachers during school vacation period, athletes off-season, news carriers under 18.	Texas Employment Commission T.E.C. Building Austin, Texas Phone: (512) 472-6251
Texas Worker's Compensation Act of 1917, as amended to 1977.	Provides prompt payment of benefits to employees or their survivors for work-related disease, injury or death, regardless of fault or cause.	All employers, except of domestic servants and farm labor.	Railway employees covered by a separate law.	Texas Industrial Accident Board L.B.J. Bldg. 111 E. 17th Street P.O. Box 12757, Capitol Station Austin, Texas 78711 Phone: (512) 475-2251 Regional offices in Dallas, Corpus Christi, El Paso, and Fort Worth.
				Division of Occupational Safety 1100 West 49th Street Austin, Texas 78756 Phone: (512) 458-7287

Appendix B

Statewide Labor-Management Organizations

Texas AFL-CIO (Texas Federation of Labor)
1106 La Vaca
P.O. Box 12727
Austin, Texas 78711
Phone: (512) 477-6195

Texas State Chamber of Commerce
Box 4304
Austin, Texas 78751
Phone: (512) 477-7030

Texas Association of Business
611-612 Three A Life Building
San Antonio, Texas 78205
Phone: (512) 227-9702

United Auto Workers—Area Office
5244 E. Grand
Dallas, Texas 75223
Phone: (214) 826-7940

International Brotherhood of Teamsters (Texas Conference)
1007 Jonelle
Dallas, Texas 75217
Phone: (214) 398-0661

Appendix C
National Labor Relations Act

The National Labor Relations Act guarantees and protects the right of workers to union organization and collective bargaining.

Covered Employment

The law applies to all enterprises whose operation affects interstate commerce, i.e., all but purely local business. The NLRB, however, assumes jurisdiction over businesses with at least:

1. $500,000 annual gross volume of business in retail trade, taxicabs, hotels and motels
2. $250,000 annual gross volume of business in public utilities and transit systems
3. $200,000 annual gross volume of business in newspapers
4. $100,000 annual gross volume of business in office buildings, radio, television, telegraph, and telephone
5. $50,000 gross annual volume of transportation or operations having nonretail, outflow or inflow, direct or indirect
6. All enterprises whose operations affect national defense

In addition, the act specifically exempts the following from protection:

1. Employees who are under the Railway Labor Act
2. Federal Reserve Bank employees
3. An individual employed by parent or spouse
4. Employees of the federal government, or any state or political subdivision thereof

5. Domestic servants
6. Agricultural laborers
7. Independent contractors who depend on profits rather than wages for their commission
8. Supervisors (i.e., those having authority to hire, discharge, discipline, direct, or adjust grievances if the exercise of authority requires independent judgment)

Rights of Employees

Employees have the right to self-organization, to form or join labor unions, and to engage in other concerted activities; to bargain collectively; and to refrain from these activities, unless a "union shop" is in effect. In order to guarantee these rights, the National Labor Relations Board (NLRB) has authority to prohibit or remedy unfair labor practices under the act, and to conduct elections to determine the representation of employees bargaining with their employer.

Representation Elections

An employer is required to bargain with the representative selected by the majority of his employees in a unit appropriate for bargaining (e.g., one plant, one employer, production and maintenance workers, or other unit grouping which reflects common worker interests).

One method of selecting a majority representative is through an election conducted by the NLRB, after a petition has been filed by the employees or an employer. A secret-ballot election is held, and the board certifies the majority choice. The employees are given a choice of one or more unions, or no union.

Unfair Labor Practices of Employers

Employers are forbidden by law to:

1. Coerce or threaten employees in the exercise of their rights under this law

2. Assist in organizing or operating a union
3. Discriminate in hiring on account of union membership or non-membership (except where union shop agreements are permitted) or against employees who have filed charges under the act
4. Refuse to bargain in good faith
5. Agree to hot-cargo contracts

Unfair Labor Practices of Unions

Labor organizations are forbidden by law to:

1. Restrain or coerce employees in their exercise of rights under the law
2. Attempt to cause discrimination for union activities
3. Refuse to bargain in good faith
4. Engage in secondary boycotts, sympathy strikes, jurisdictional disputes
5. Charge excessive or discriminatory initiation fees
6. Attempt to cause an employer to pay for goods or services not performed (i.e., featherbedding)
7. Engage in organizational and recognition picketing
8. Agree to hot-cargo contracts

Union Shop

A union and an employer may sign an agreement requiring all employees to join the union, except in states (e.g., Texas) where such agreements are forbidden by state law. The agreement must provide a 30-day grace period (7 days in the construction industry). An employee may be discharged for lack of union membership only if he has failed to pay his union dues.

Conciliation of Labor Disputes

The steps required to change or terminate a contract are: (1) notification of the other party at least 60 days before the contract termination date; (2) an offer to meet with the other party; (3) notification of the Federal Mediation and Conciliation Service if no agreement has been reached within 30 days after the notice has been served, and (4) continuation without strike or lockout until 60 days after the notice was given or until the contract expires. Any employee who engages in a strike within the 60-day period shall lose his status as an employee for the purpose of this act (protection against employer unfair labor practices).

When a strike or lockout affecting a substantial part of an industry might imperil the national health or safety, the President of the United States may appoint a board of inquiry. Upon receiving their report of the dispute the President may direct the attorney general to enjoin the strike or lockout. If the parties to the dispute have not settled their differences at the end of 60 days, the board of inquiry shall report to the President the current position of each party and the employer's last offer. The NLRB will conduct a poll among employees within 15 days on whether they wish to accept the final offer of settlement. The results of the poll are certified to the attorney general within 5 days. The injunction is discharged, and the President submits a report and recommendations to Congress.

Procedures for conciliation of labor disputes in the health care industry were established in the 1974 amendments to the Act (Section 8[d], 8[g], 19, and 23).

Political Contributions

It is unlawful for any labor organization to make a contribution or expenditure in connection with a presidential or congressional election, or in connection with any primary election or political convention held to select candidates for national office, or for any candidate, political committee, or other person to accept any such contribution.

Administration and Enforcement

The National Labor Relations Board administers the act. Petitions for elections and charges of unfair labor practices should be filed with the nearest regional office.

Appendix D

Labor-Management Reporting and Disclosure Act

The purpose of the act is to eliminate or prevent improper practices by unions, employers, and labor-relations consultants which distort or defeat the policies of the National Labor Relations Act and the Railway Labor Act.

Covered Employment

Employers are covered who are engaged in an industry which affects interstate commerce and which (1) is an employer within the meaning of any federal law relating to employees or (2) deals with a union engaged in an industry affecting commerce. Specifically excluded are the U.S. government, state government, and political subdivisions of the states.

Labor organizations are covered if they are (1) the certified representative of the employees under the National Labor Relation Act or the Railway Labor Act, (2) a national or a local union representing or actively seeking to represent employees of an employer engaged in interstate commerce, (3) a conference, committee, board, or council subordinate to a union covered under the law. State and local central bodies are excluded.

Title I-Bill of Rights

Every member of a union has the following rights and privileges:

1. Equal rights to nominate candidates for union office, vote in union elections and referendums, attend membership meetings, and participate in discussions and voting on union business, subject to reasonable rules in the union's constitution and by-laws.
2. Freedom of speech in and out of union meetings, subject to the union's reasonable rules.
3. Dues, fees, and assessments can be levied only by majority vote of members in a local union or delegates to a national union. Federations like the AFL-CIO are excluded.
4. Right to sue the union or its officers after exhausting reasonable hearing procedures within the union.
5. Immunity to fine, suspension, or expulsion by a union except for nonpayment of dues, without a full and fair hearing.
6. Right to bring action in a U.S. district court, under Title I.
7. Right to receive, upon request, from the union local a copy of each collective bargaining agreement.

Title II-Reporting Requirements

Labor organizations are required to file with the secretary of labor (1) copies of their constitution and by-laws (as previously required under section 9[f] [A] of the Taft-Hartley Act) and (2) annual financial reports of receipts and disbursements, assets and liabilities, payments to each employee in excess of $10,000 per year, and loans made by the union. This information must be made available to all of their members. Union officers must report "conflict of interest" transactions.

Employers must report annually to the secretary of labor any payments or loans to unions, and expenditures to employees or labor-relations consultants where the purpose is to interfere with the right of employees to organize and bargain collectively.

Labor-relations consultants must file reports of their agreements and reimbursements for activities where the object is to persuade workers in their exercise of the right to organize and bargain collectively, or to furnish an employer with information concerning employee or union activities in connection with labor disputes.

The information contained in the above reports is public information. The secretary of labor may publish the information, or studies based thereon. He must furnish copies of reports on payment of the cost of the service. No charge is made for copies to state agencies.

Title III-Trusteeships

Trusteeships assumed over a subordinate labor organization must be reported to the secretary of labor semiannually, and may not continue for longer than 18 months. The purpose of the trusteeship is limited to correct corruption or financial malpractice, to assure the performance of collective bargaining agreements, to restore democratic procedures, or otherwise to carry out the legitimate objects of the union.

Title IV-Elections

National unions must hold elections by secret ballot at least every five years, and officers of intermediate union bodies are to be elected at least every four years by secret ballot. Local unions must elect officers at least every three years. Every candidate has the right to inspect but not to copy a list of all members of the local union. Similar privileges regarding distribution of campaign literature must be accorded all candidates. Neither unions nor employee funds can be used to promote any candidate.

Title V-Judiciary Safeguards for Labor Organizations

Union officers must hold the union's money and property solely for the benefit of the union and its members. All union officers must be bonded in an amount at least 10% of the funds they handle, but not less than $1,000 in a local union or $10,000 in a national union.

A union may not make loans to officers or employees in excess of $2,000.

No person may serve as a labor-relations consultant or union officer or employee (except clerical or custodial) if he is, or within the preceding five years has been, a member of the Communist Party (found unconstitutional, *U.S.* vs. *Brown,* 1965), a convicted felon, or a convicted violator of Title II or Title III.

References

Bureau of National Affairs, Inc., *BNA Labor Relations Reporter. State Laws. 4A.*, Washington, D.C., (loose-leaf papers).

Commerce Clearing House. *1977 Guidebook to Fair Employment Practices.* Chicago: Commerce Clearing House, 1977.

U.S. Department of Health, Education, and Welfare. Social Security Administration. *Your Medicare Handbook.* Washington, D.C.: Government Printing Office, 1977.

U.S. Department of Health, Education, and Welfare. Social Security Administration. *Your Social Security.* Washington, D.C.: Government Printing Office, 1977.

U.S. Department of Labor. Occupational Safety and Health Administration. *All About OSHA. OSHA Publications and Training Materials.* Washington, D.C.: Government Printing Office, 1976.

U.S. Department of the Treasury. Internal Revenue Service. *1973 Circular E. Employer's Tax Guide.* Publication 15 (See also Supplements). Washington, D.C.: Government Printing Office, 1977.

U.S. Department of the Treasury. Internal Revenue Service. *1977 Circular A. Agricultural Employer's Tax Guide.* Publication 51. Washington, D.C.: Government Printing Office, 1977.

Vernon's Annotated Revised Civil Statutes of the State of Texas. Vol. 15 (Labor). St. Paul, Minn., West Publishing Co., 1971 (with Cumulative Annual Pocket Part).

Index

E

F

G-J

L

M

N-O

Cases Index

NOTES

NOTES

NOTES